50 birthday cakes

for kids

D0567654

4/16

50 birthday cakes
for kids

Annie Rigg

photography by Sandra Lane

RYLAND PETERS & SMALL
LONDON • NEW YORK

To my godchildren, Alec, Izzie, Albie and Tom Tom

Senior designer Megan Smith
Senior editor Céline Hughes
Head of production Patricia Harrington
Art director Leslie Harrington
Publishing director Alison Starling

Prop stylist Liz Belton
Indexer Hilary Bird
Diagrams Ray Betts

Originally published in 2009.
Revised edition published in 2012.
This edition published in 2016
by Ryland Peters & Small
20–21 Jockey's Fields
London WC1R 4BW
and
341 E 116th St
New York, NY 10029
www.rylandpeters.com

10 9 8 7 6 5 4 3 2 1

Text © Annie Rigg 2009, 2012, 2016

Design and photographs
© Ryland Peters & Small 2009, 2012, 2016

ISBN: 978-1-84975-732-4

Printed and bound in China

The author's moral rights have been asserted. All rights reserved. No part of this publication may be reproduced, stored in a retrieval system or transmitted in any form or by any means, electronic, mechanical, photocopying or otherwise, without the prior permission of the publisher.

A CIP record for this book is available from the British Library. The first edition of this book was catalogued as follows:

Library of Congress Cataloging-in-Publication Data

Rigg, Annie.
  Birthday cakes for kids / Annie Rigg ; photography by Sandra Lane.
    p. cm.
  Includes index.
  ISBN 978-1-84597-833-4
  1. Cake decorating. 2. Birthday cakes. I. Title.
  TX771.2.R54 2009
  641.8'6539--dc22

                              2008047466

• All spoon measurements are level, unless otherwise specified.
• Ovens should be preheated to the specified temperature. Recipes in this book were tested using a regular oven. If using a fan-assisted oven, follow the manufacturer's instructions for adjusting temperatures.
• All eggs are UK medium/US large, unless otherwise specified. Recipes containing raw or partially cooked egg should not be served to the very young, very old, anyone with a compromised immune system or pregnant women.

contents

the star of the show

One of the most important elements of any child's birthday party has to be the cake. Most people can easily remember their favourite birthday cake from childhood and the excitement in choosing a cake every year. Whether you make the same cake every time or something completely different, a homemade cake simply can't be beaten both for the joy it gives children and the satisfaction of knowing that it's all your work.

I'm lucky to have eager guinea pigs in my small tribe of godchildren, who provided plenty of inspiration for the cakes in this book. I have loved baking since I was a little girl and I hope that they too will soon discover what fun there is to be had in the kitchen sticking, layering, frosting and decorating. The results are so rewarding. And who knows, they may even start coming up with some imaginative creations of their own.

Whatever your level of baking skills there's a cake here to suit everyone. There are also a few basic guidelines on pages 10 and 16–19 to help you get the best results whenever you bake.

Most of the cakes in this book can be made ahead of time and can be kept for up to 2 days (undecorated), well wrapped in clingfilm/plastic wrap, or frozen undecorated and defrosted the day before the party. Cupcakes keep well in the freezer and defrost quickly, making them an easy and convenient option. In fact, cupcakes are a great starting point if you are nervous about your baking skills.

If you don't want to test your construction skills then choose a cake that can be shaped by cutting around a template rather than one that requires measuring and layering. Most of the cakes here are easy for the novice baker – just remember to allow yourself plenty of time to complete the frosting and final decorations. Remember that any imperfections can be cunningly disguised under a layer of frosting and sprinkles.

No matter which cake you choose to make for your child's birthday, you can be sure of smiles of delight when they are presented with a home-baked creation. And if at first you feel unsure about assembling, layering and decorating, there's always the old favourite – chocolate cake. Don't forget the candles!

the basics

basic vanilla cake

This is the most basic vanilla cake mixture, which can be adapted to introduce different flavours (see end of recipe). It is used in many of the recipes in this book as it makes a good base for cakes which need to be cut up and re-assembled, and it tends to be liked by most kids. I have provided four quantities to suit individual recipes but the method remains the same regardless of the quantity you use. For best results I suggest using an electric freestanding mixer. Before you start baking make sure all ingredients are at room temperature, the oven is preheated with the oven shelf in the correct position and the relevant cake pans have been prepared. The oven temperatures given throughout the book are for a conventional oven; if you are using a fan oven, adjust the temperature according to the manufacturer's instructions.

EXTRA LARGE

350 g/3 sticks unsalted
butter, room temperature
350 g/2 cups (caster) sugar
6 large eggs, beaten
2 teaspoons vanilla extract
350 g/3 cups plain/cake
flour
5 teaspoons baking powder
4–5 tablespoons milk,
room temperature

LARGE

250 g/2 sticks unsalted
butter, room temperature
250 g/1¼ cups (caster)
sugar
4 large eggs, beaten
1 teaspoon vanilla extract
250 g/2¼ cups plain/cake
flour
4 teaspoons baking powder
3–4 tablespoons milk,
room temperature

MEDIUM

175 g/1½ sticks unsalted
butter, room temperature
175 g/1 cup (caster) sugar
3 large eggs, beaten
1 teaspoon vanilla extract
175 g/1½ cups plain/cake
flour
3 teaspoons baking powder
3 tablespoons milk,
room temperature

SMALL

125 g/1 stick unsalted
butter, room temperature
125 g/½ cup (caster) sugar
2 large eggs, beaten
½ teaspoon vanilla extract
125 g/1 cup plus 2
tablespoons plain/all-
purpose flour
2 teaspoons baking powder
2 tablespoons milk,
room temperature

Preheat the oven to 180°C (350°F) Gas 4.

Cream the butter and sugar in an electric mixer or with
a handheld electric whisk until pale, light and fluffy, about
2–3 minutes. Very gradually add the beaten eggs, mixing well
between each addition and scraping down the bowl with
a rubber spatula from time to time. Stir in the vanilla extract.

Sift together the flour and baking powder and add to the cake
mixture in 2 batches, mixing until smooth. Add the milk and
mix until smooth.

Revert to the relevant cake recipe and continue as instructed.

ALTERNATIVE FLAVOURS

Basic chocolate: substitute 4 tablespoons unsweetened cocoa
for the same quantity of flour in the Extra Large mixture,
3 tablespoons in the Large, 2 in the Medium and 1 in the
Small cake.

Lemon or orange: substitute the grated zest of an unwaxed
lemon or orange for the vanilla extract.

These shapes will keep un-iced for 3 days in an airtight container. Once iced, they should be eaten within 24 hours.

gingerbread shapes

175 g/1⅓ cups plain/all-
purpose flour
¼ teaspoon bicarbonate of/
baking soda
a pinch of salt
1 generous teaspoon
ground ginger
1 teaspoon ground cinnamon
a large pinch of ground
allspice
75 g/5 tablespooons
unsalted butter, cold
and diced
75 g/⅓ cup (caster) sugar
2 generous tablespoons
golden/light corn syrup
1 large egg yolk

*several baking sheets, lined
with baking parchment*

MAKES ABOUT 10–12

Sift the flour, bicarbonate of/baking soda, salt, ginger, cinnamon and allspice into a bowl or an electric freestanding mixer.

Rub the butter into the dry ingredients (or process) until the mixture resembles breadcrumbs. Add the sugar and mix.

Beat the golden/corn syrup and egg yolk together, add to the bowl and mix to a smooth dough, kneading very lightly.

Flatten into a disc, cover with clingfilm/plastic wrap and refrigerate for 30 minutes.

Preheat the oven to 180°C (350°F) Gas 4.

On a lightly floured work surface, roll the gingerbread dough out to a thickness of about 4 mm/¼ inch. Stamp out your desired shapes and arrange on the prepared baking sheets. Re-roll and stamp out any trimmings.

Bake on the middle shelf of the preheated oven for 10–12 minutes until firm and starting to darken very slightly at the edges. Let cool slightly on the baking sheets, then transfer to a wire cooling rack.

These cookies will keep un-iced for 3 days in an airtight container. Once iced, they should be eaten within 24 hours.

shortbread

225 g/2 sticks unsalted butter, room temperature
275 g/1⅓ cups (caster) sugar
1 large egg, beaten
½ teaspoon vanilla extract
a pinch of salt

325 g/1½ cups plain/all-purpose flour

several baking sheets, lined with baking parchment

MAKES ABOUT 10–12

Cream the butter and sugar in an electric mixer or with a handheld electric whisk until pale, light and fluffy, about 2–3 minutes. Add the beaten egg, vanilla extract and a pinch of salt and mix until combined.

Gradually add the flour and mix until incorporated. Flatten the dough into a disc, cover with clingfilm/plastic wrap and refrigerate for a couple of hours.

On a lightly floured work surface, roll the shortbread dough out to a thickness of about 4 mm/¼ inch. Stamp out your desired shapes and arrange on the prepared baking sheets. Re-roll and stamp out any trimmings. Refrigerate for a further 15 minutes.

Preheat the oven to 180°C (350°F) Gas 4.

Bake on the middle shelf of the preheated oven for 10–12 minutes until pale golden and firm to the touch. Let cool slightly on the baking sheets, then transfer to a wire cooling rack.

Buttercream is a dream to pipe and spread over cakes and chocolate fudge frosting is good enough to eat straight from the bowl! When using meringue frosting it helps to freeze the cake base for 1 hour first. This makes the surface of the cake firmer and crumbs are less likely to spoil the clean, white finish of the frosting. Once the frosting has been cooked, work quickly using a palette knife dipped in hot water to make spreading easier. Glacé icing is ideal for decorating cookies. I use an egg white to make it set firmly but you can use cold water instead (but the icing will not set as stiffly).

buttercream

350 g/3 sticks unsalted
   butter, room temperature
700 g/4⅔ cups icing/
   confectioners' sugar,
   sifted
vanilla extract, optional

Cream the butter in an electric mixer or in a large bowl with a handheld electric whisk until really soft. Gradually beat in the icing/confectioners' sugar until pale and smooth. Add a few drops of vanilla extract, if using.

chocolate fudge frosting

350 g/12 oz. dark/
   bittersweet chocolate,
   roughly chopped
225 g/2 sticks unsalted
   butter
225 ml/⅔ cup milk
1 teaspoon vanilla extract
450 g/3¼ cups icing/
   confectioners' sugar, sifted

Melt the chocolate and butter together in a heatproof bowl set over a pan of barely simmering water (do not let the base of the bowl touch the water). Stir until melted and smooth, then set aside to cool slightly.

In another bowl, whisk together the milk, vanilla extract and icing/confectioners' sugar until smooth. Add the cooled chocolate mixture and stir until smooth. Let the frosting set and thicken up slightly before use.

meringue frosting

250 g/1¼ cups (caster)
   sugar
4 large egg whites
a pinch of salt

Set a medium-large heatproof bowl over a pan of barely simmering water (do not let the base of the bowl touch the water). Put the sugar, egg whites, salt and 2 tablespoons water into the bowl and using a handheld electric whisk, whisk on medium speed so that the sugar completely dissolves into the egg whites. Continue to whisk until the meringue is white, soft and pillowy. Increase the speed to high and whisk for another minute until the meringue is hot, stiff and glossy.

Remove from the heat and continue whisking for a further minute until the meringue has cooled slightly. Working very quickly and using a palette knife dipped in hot water, spread the frosting over the cake.

glacé icing

1 large egg white
1 tablespoon freshly
   squeezed lemon juice
250–300 g/1¾–2 cups icing/
   confectioners' sugar, sifted

Beat the egg white with the lemon juice in a medium bowl until combined. Gradually add the icing/confectioners' sugar until the icing is smooth and the consistency of slightly thickened double/heavy cream and will coat the back of a spoon. Cover with clingfilm/plastic wrap until ready to use.

decoration

SUGAR/GUM PASTE (REGAL ICE) AND ROYAL ICING
Sugar/gum paste (Regal Ice) and royal icing are ideal for modelling and cutting into decorative shapes. They are available ready-to-roll – simply follow the manufacturer's instructions. They can be found in white in many supermarkets, but for a wider range of colours, go to a cake decorating supply store.

FONDANT ICING
Fondant icing is also readily available and sold in blocks.

It requires rolling out on a work surface that has been lightly dusted with icing/confectioners' sugar. Use food colouring pastes to tint the icing to your desired shade. Once iced, cover the cake and leave it for at least 4 hours to allow the icing to dry.

READY-ROLLED ICING
Ready-rolled royal and fondant icing usually come in a circle ready for icing a round cake. I would suggest covering the cake first in a thin layer of either buttercream or marzipan.

WRITING ICING

Ready-to-use writing icing tubes are widely available in the baking sections of most supermarkets and come in a selection of colours but mainly red, green, black and yellow. They are ideal when small amounts of icing are required for writing letters, numbers and words on cakes and for drawing outlines. They are small and easy for children to use without getting too messy! Look out for gel and sparkly writing icing too.

PIPING BAGS

Even if your icing skills aren't in the professional league, a piping bag and selection of nozzles/tips are useful for creating simple but effective decorations. Fit a piping bag with a star nozzle/tip and fill with buttercream to create rosette or flower shapes as a simple way of covering cakes.

TINTING WITH FOOD COLOURING

Food colouring pastes are easier to use than the standard liquid colours and come in a vast selection of colours. They can be used to tint ready-to-roll icing, fondant icing and buttercream, and are generally available from cake decorating supply stores and online suppliers. A very tiny amount gives a good colour without watering down the icing. Add the paste very gradually using the point of a cocktail stick/toothpick or wooden skewer and mix well or knead into the icing before adding more until you have the shade you're after.

SPRINKLES AND CANDY

Most supermarkets carry a wide range of edible decorating sprinkles in the home baking section, ranging from sprinkles to edible silver balls and shapes especially for Halloween and Christmas. Specialty cake decorating stores generally stock a wide range of sprinkles in many shapes and colours. Sweet shops and candy stores are a fantastic source for cake decorations – liquorice shapes, chocolate buttons, sugar-coated chocolate drops and marshmallows can all be used to great effect on cakes.

basic techniques

1

2

3

4

1 CUTTING

Always use a long-bladed, serrated knife to slice cakes into layers for filling. Put the cake on a clean, flat work surface. Hold the knife level and horizontal and use a gentle sawing action to slice the cake evenly. Keep your fingers out of the way!

2 FILLING

Cakes can be filled with a variety of fillings such as jam, buttercream or whipped fresh cream. If necessary, cut a thin slice off the top of the cakes to make the surfaces flat. Lay the bottom layer on the work surface or serving plate and spoon the filling on to the cake. Spread evenly using a long palette knife. Top with another layer of cake and repeat as necessary.

3 CUTTING THE CAKE BASE FOR THE PIRATE SHIP (PAGE 74)

Lay the cake on the work surface with the long edge closest to you. Trim the edges of the cake to make a neat rectangle and save any trimmings to snack on. Using a long-bladed knife, cut a rectangle, about 9 x 23 cm/ 4 x 9 inches, from one end of the cake. Slice the remaining cake in half to give 2 rectangles roughly 11 x 23 cm/4¼ x 8½ inches.

4 STACKING THE PIECES OF CAKE FOR THE PIRATE SHIP

Stack the 2 larger rectangles one on top of the other. Cut the small rectangle in half and lay one piece at each end of the stacked cakes.

5 SHAPING THE PIECES OF CAKE FOR THE PIRATE SHIP
Slice a triangular wedge from the front of the cake, on both sides, to make the prow of the pirate ship. Once you have the cake cut and assembled you can secure the sections with wooden skewers or brush a little warmed jam between the layers to stick them together. The pirate ship is now ready to be frosted. Remember to pull out any skewers before serving the cake.

6 PAPER TEMPLATES
Draw or trace your desired shape on to a sheet of paper (for example greaseproof paper or baking parchment) the same size as your uncut cake. Lay the template on the cake and, using a small, sharp knife, cut around the template. This is easier if the cake has been make the day before and if possible chilled in the fridge for a couple of hours first.

7 FROSTING
When frosting a cake that has been cut out from a template, refrigerate the cake for 1–2 hours first. Alternatively, you can brush the surface of the cake with a little warmed, sifted jam first. This helps prevent crumbs mixing into the frosting as you spread it over the cut edges. A selection of palette knives in different sizes is useful. I often use small palette knives bought from artists' supply stores for the trickier shapes.

8 PIPING DECORATION
Once your cake has been covered in frosting, the fun starts! With a steady hand, pipe outlines on to the frosting to clearly define the shapes which can later be filled in with another colour of frosting. Have a clear idea of exactly where you want to draw the lines before starting. You may find it easier to mark out the lines using the point of a cocktail stick/toothpick first.

diagrams

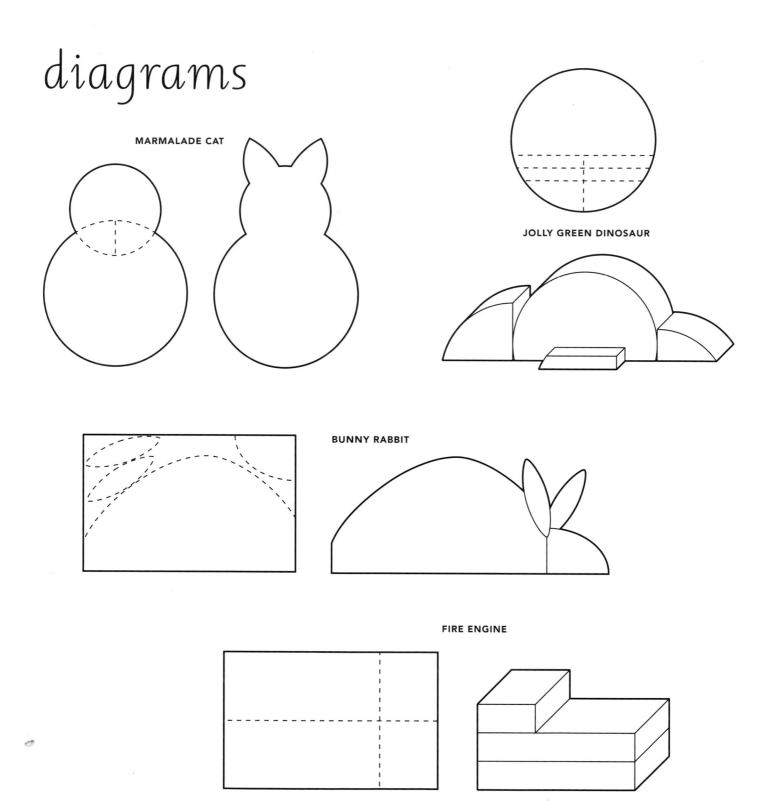

MARMALADE CAT

JOLLY GREEN DINOSAUR

BUNNY RABBIT

FIRE ENGINE

ROCKET SHIP

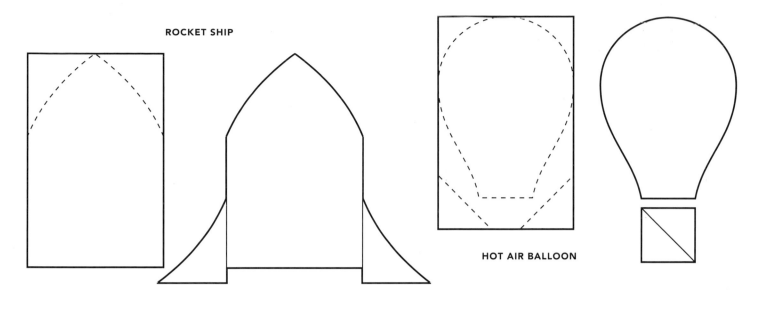

HOT AIR BALLOON

BIG GREEN TRACTOR

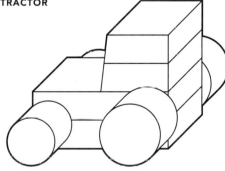

STEAM TRAIN SET

FAIRYTALE CASTLE

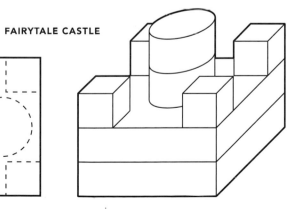

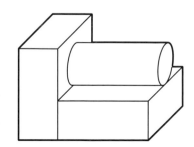

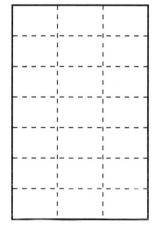

simple cakes

This cake keeps really well and can be made a day in advance and kept undecorated either wrapped up or in an airtight container until ready to serve.

carrot & coconut cake

75 g/½ cup shelled pecans

375 g/2¾ cups plain/all-purpose flour

2 teaspoons baking powder

1 teaspoon bicarbonate of/baking soda

½ teaspoon ground cinnamon

3 large eggs

375 ml/1½ cups groundnut oil

450 g/2¼ cups (unrefined caster) sugar

4 tablespoons milk

1 teaspoon vanilla extract

500 g/1 lb. carrots, grated

grated zest of 1 orange

125 g/1 cup desiccated coconut

100 g/3½ oz. marzipan

orange food colouring paste

angelica

FROSTING

450 g/1 lb. cream cheese

2–3 big tablespoons honey

2 x 20-cm/8-inch round cake pans, greased and baselined with greased baking parchment

SERVES 8–10

Preheat the oven to 180°C (350°F) Gas 4.

Put the pecans on a baking sheet and toast in the preheated oven for 7 minutes. Let cool slightly, then roughly chop. Leave the oven on for the cake.

Sift the flour, baking powder, bicarbonate of/baking soda and cinnamon together into a bowl and set aside.

In another bowl, whisk together the eggs, groundnut oil, sugar, milk and vanilla extract and mix until smooth. Add the carrots, orange zest, desiccated coconut and pecans and mix well. Add the dry ingredients and fold in using a large spoon or rubber spatula until thoroughly combined.

Divide the mixture between the prepared cake pans and bake on the middle shelf of the preheated oven for about 40 minutes, or until a skewer inserted into the middle of the cakes comes out clean. Let the cakes cool in the pans for 10 minutes before turning out on to wire cooling racks. Turn the cakes the right way up and let cool completely.

To make the frosting, beat the cream cheese and honey together until smooth. Place one of the carrot cakes on a large plate and spread half the frosting over the it. Cover with the second cake and the remaining frosting.

To make the carrots, tint the marzipan orange with the orange food colouring paste (page 17). Break off ½–1 teaspoon marzipan and roll between your hands into a carrot shape. Repeat with the remaining marzipan. Using the blunt end of a wooden skewer push a small hole into the top of each carrot. Let the carrots dry overnight on a sheet of baking parchment in an airtight container.

Cut the angelica into very fine matchsticks about 2 cm/1 inch long and push into the top of each carrot. Decorate the cake with the carrots and an optional chocolate rabbit!

Banoffee pie in a cake! Dulce de leche is a hugely popular ingredient in Argentinian desserts and sweets. It is now widely available in most supermarkets and is sometimes called Banoffee Toffee.

banana & toffee cake

325 g/2½ cups plain/all-purpose flour

1½ teaspoons baking powder

1 teaspoon bicarbonate of/baking soda

3 ripe bananas

4 tablespoons sour cream, room temperature

1 teaspoon vanilla extract

175 g/1½ sticks unsalted butter, room temperature

125 g/½ cup soft/packed light brown sugar

100 g/½ cup (caster) sugar

4 large eggs, beaten

100 g/3½ oz. dark/semisweet chocolate, grated

FROSTING

400 g/1⅔ cups mascarpone

400 g/1⅔ cups dulce de leche

2 x 20-cm/8-inch round cake pans, greased and baselined with greased baking parchment

SERVES 10

Preheat the oven to 180°C (350°F) Gas 4.

Sift the flour, baking powder and bicarbonate of/baking soda together into a bowl and set aside.

Mash the bananas in a bowl and mix in the sour cream and vanilla extract.

Cream the butter and sugar in an electric mixer or with a handheld electric whisk until pale, light and fluffy. Gradually add the eggs, mixing well between each addition and scraping down the bowl with a rubber spatula from time to time.

Add the dry ingredients in 2 or 3 batches with the mixer or whisk on a slow speed, mixing well until thoroughly incorporated. Fold in the banana mixture using a rubber spatula.

Divide the mixture between the prepared cake pans and bake on the middle shelf of the preheated oven for about 35 minutes, or until a skewer inserted into the middle of the cakes comes out clean. Let the cakes cool in the pans for 10 minutes before turning out on to wire cooling racks. Turn the cakes the right way up and let cool completely.

When you are ready to assemble the cake, take a large, serrated knife and slice each cake in half horizontally to give 4 even layers.

Place one cake layer on a serving plate and spread with one-quarter of the mascarpone. Carefully spread or drizzle one-quarter of the dulce de leche over the mascarpone followed by one-quarter of the grated chocolate. Continue layering up in this manner, ending with a layer of chocolate.

This cake keeps really well wrapped up or in an airtight container and can be made a day in advance and frosted on the day of the party. Don't be tempted to over-swirl the mixtures or the marble effect will be less dramatic.

marble cake

75 g/2½ oz. dark/semisweet chocolate, chopped
175 g/1⅓ cups plain/all-purpose flour
1 big teaspoon baking powder
175 g/1½ sticks unsalted butter, room temperature
200 g/1 cup (caster) sugar
1 teaspoon vanilla extract
4 large eggs, beaten
chocolate sprinkles

FROSTING
125 g/4 oz. dark/semisweet chocolate, chopped
75 g/5 tablespoons unsalted butter
75 ml/5 tablespoons milk
½ teaspoon vanilla extract
150 g/1¼ cups icing/confectioners' sugar

20 x 13-cm/9 x 5 x 3-inch loaf pan, greased and base and ends lined with greased baking parchment

SERVES 8–10

Preheat the oven to 180°C (350°F) Gas 4.

Put the chocolate in a heatproof bowl set over a pan of barely simmering water (do not let the base of the bowl touch the water). Stir until melted and smooth, then set aside to cool slightly.

Sift the flour and baking powder together.

Cream the butter and sugar in an electric mixer or with a handheld electric whisk until pale, light and fluffy. Stir in the vanilla extract. Gradually add the eggs, mixing well between each addition and scraping down the bowl with a rubber spatula from time to time.

Add the dry ingredients and mix until smooth. Spoon one-third of the mixture into the melted chocolate. Mix until smooth.

Using a tablespoon, drop alternate spoonfuls of vanilla and chocolate mixture into the prepared loaf pan. Once all of the mixture has been used, give the pan a sharp tap on the work surface to level the mixture. To create a marble effect, drag the blade of a table knife through the mixture to create swirls, taking care not to over-swirl the mixture.

Bake on the middle shelf of the preheated oven for about 1 hour, or until a skewer inserted into the middle of the cake comes out clean. Let the cake cool in the pan for 10 minutes before turning out on to a wire cooling rack. Turn the cake the right way up and let cool completely.

To make the frosting, put the chocolate and butter in a heatproof bowl set over a pan of barely simmering water (do not let the base of the bowl touch the water). Stir until melted and smooth, then set aside to cool slightly.

In another bowl, whisk together the milk, vanilla extract and icing/confectioners' sugar until smooth. Add the cooled chocolate mixture and stir until smooth. Let the frosting set and thicken up slightly before use.

Once the cake is completely cold, top with the frosting and decorate with your choice of assorted chocolate sprinkles.

This is a deliciously light lemon layer cake. Go wild with the decorations and use lots of different varieties and colours of candies. The cake can be assembled and frosted in advance but don't add the candies until about 1–2 hours before serving otherwise they will soften and bleed into the frosting.

lemon cake

400 g/3 cups plain/all-
    purpose flour
1 tablespoon baking powder
225 g/2 cups unsalted
    butter, room temperature
225 g/1 cup (caster) sugar
4 large eggs, beaten
250 ml/1 cup sour cream,
    room temperature
grated zest of 2 unwaxed
    lemons and juice of 1
assorted candy

FROSTING
350 g/3 sticks unsalted
    butter, room temperature
600 g/4 cups icing/
    confectioners' sugar, sifted
4 tablespoons lemon curd

*2 x 20-cm/8-inch round
cake pans, greased and
baselined with greased
baking parchment*

SERVES 8–10

Preheat the oven to 180°C (350°F) Gas 4.

Sift the flour and baking powder together.

Cream the butter and sugar in an electric mixer or with a handheld electric whisk until pale, light and fluffy. Gradually add the eggs, mixing well between each addition and scraping down the bowl with a rubber spatula from time to time.

With the mixer or whisk on a low speed add the dry ingredients and sour cream alternately to the mixture in batches. Add the lemon zest and juice and mix until smooth.

Divide the mixture evenly between the prepared cake pans and bake on the middle shelf of the preheated oven for about 35 minutes, or until a skewer inserted into the middle of the cakes comes out clean. Let the cakes cool in the pans for 10 minutes before

turning out on to wire cooling racks. Turn the cakes the right way up and let cool completely before decorating.

To make the frosting, cream the butter and sugar until smooth and pale. Add the lemon curd and mix again until smooth.

When you are ready to assemble the cake, take a large, serrated knife and slice each cake in half horizontally to give 4 even layers.

Place one cake layer on a serving plate and spread with 2 big tablespoons of frosting. Top with another cake layer and frosting. Repeat until you have 4 layers of cake and 3 of frosting. Cover the top and sides of the whole cake with the remaining frosting, spreading evenly with a palette knife.

Decorate the cake with your choice of assorted candy.

This recipe has been adapted from one by Emily Luchetti in her fabulous *Stars Desserts* cookbook which is now sadly out of print.

fantastic chocolate cake

125 g/1 cup cocoa

400 g/3 cups plain/all-purpose flour

2 teaspoons baking powder

1½ teaspoons bicarbonate of/baking soda

150 g/10 tablespoons unsalted butter, room temperature

500 g/2½ cups (caster) sugar

3 large eggs, beaten

300 ml/1¼ cups buttermilk, room temperature

FROSTING

350 g/12 oz. dark/bittersweet chocolate, chopped

225 g/15 tablespoons unsalted butter

225 ml/1 cup milk

1 teaspoon vanilla extract

450 g/4 cups icing/confectioners' sugar, sifted

10-cm/4-inch, 18-cm/7-inch and 23-cm/9-inch round cake pans, greased and baselined with greased baking parchment

SERVES 14–16

Preheat the oven to 180°C (350°F) Gas 4.

Put the cocoa and 250 ml/1 cup boiling water in a medium bowl, whisk until smooth and set aside to cool down.

Sift the flour, baking powder and bicarbonate of/baking soda together into a bowl.

Cream the butter and sugar in an electric mixer or with a handheld electric whisk until pale, light and fluffy. Gradually add the eggs, mixing well between each addition and scraping down the bowl with a rubber spatula from time to time.

Add the dry ingredients and buttermilk alternately to the mixture in batches. Add the cocoa mixture and stir until thoroughly combined and the batter is smooth.

Divide the mixture between the prepared cake pans. Bake in the preheated oven until a skewer inserted into the middle of the cakes comes out clean – about 25 minutes for the smallest cake, 30–35 minutes for the medium cake, and 40–45 minutes for the largest cake. Let the cakes cool in the pans for 10 minutes before turning out on to wire cooling racks. Turn the cakes the right way up and let cool completely.

To make the frosting, melt the chocolate and butter in a heatproof bowl set over a pan of barely simmering water (do not let the base of the bowl touch the water). Stir until melted and smooth and set aside to cool slightly.

In another bowl, whisk together the milk, vanilla extract and icing/confectioners' sugar until smooth. Add the cooled chocolate mixture and stir until smooth. Let the frosting set and thicken up slightly before using.

Using a long, serrated knife cut all 3 cakes in half horizontally. Place one layer of the largest cake on a serving plate and spread with a couple of tablespoons of the frosting. Cover with the other half of the cake. Repeat with the remaining cakes, stacking one on top of the other, from large to small. Cover the whole cake with frosting, spreading it evenly with a palette knife.

If you don't want to make nine building blocks, this cake can easily be cut into four larger squares instead. Beware that the cake needs to be left overnight before the party (in an airtight container) to give the icing time to set.

building blocks

2 quantities Medium Basic
  Vanilla Cake (page 11)
6 tablespoons raspberry
  jam, sifted
3 tablespoons Buttercream
  (page 14), optional
500 g/1 lb. marzipan
500 g/1 lb. ready-to-roll
  royal icing
food colouring pastes
  of your choice

2 x 20-cm/8-inch square
  cake pans, greased and
  baselined with greased
  baking parchment
small letter or number
  cutters
ribbons

MAKES 9

Preheat the oven to 180°C (350°F) Gas 4.

Make the 2 quantities of Vanilla Cake and divide between the prepared cake pans. Bake on the middle shelf of the preheated oven for 35–40 minutes, or until a skewer inserted into the middle of the cakes comes out clean. Let the cakes cool in the pans for 10 minutes before turning out on to wire cooling racks. Turn the cakes the right way up and let cool completely.

Level off the tops of the cakes with a sharp knife. Sandwich the cakes together with 2 tablespoons each of jam and buttercream, if using. Trim off the edges so that the cake has completely even sides. Cut the cake into 9 blocks. Heat the remaining jam in a small saucepan until runny, sift, then use to brush the top and sides of each block.

Divide the marzipan into 9 even pieces. Dust the work surface with icing/confectioners' sugar and roll out each piece of marzipan into a square no thicker than 2 mm/1⁄16 inch, and large enough to cover each block. Cover the tops and sides of the blocks with marzipan,

smoothing the surface with sugar-dusted hands. Set aside for at least 1 hour.

If using more than one food colouring, divide up the royal icing and tint each portion with your chosen colouring paste(s) (page 17). Remember that you need 9 equal pieces of icing at the end to cover your blocks. Cover with clingfilm/plastic wrap whichever icing you're not about to use. Cut the remaining icing into your chosen number of even pieces. Lightly dust the work surface with more sugar and roll each piece of icing into a square no thicker than 2 mm/1⁄16 inch, and large enough to cover each whole block. Very lightly brush each block with cooled boiled water. Cover the tops and sides of the blocks with the icing, smoothing the surface with sugar-dusted hands. Trim off the excess. Repeat with any other coloured icing and remaining blocks.

Thinly roll out the last of the icing and use to stamp out letters or numbers. Very lightly brush with cold water and stick to the sides and top of each cake. Let the cakes dry overnight before decorating with ribbons.

Keep any leftovers from the trimmings of this cake and use in a trifle or for popping into lunchboxes. When you are a more confident baker, try making other numbers.

number '5' cake

2 quantities Large Basic
   Vanilla Cake (page 11)
1 quantity Buttercream
   (page 14)
blue food colouring paste

23-cm/9-inch round cake
   pan and 20-cm/8-inch
   square cake pan, greased
   and baselined with
   greased baking
   parchment
7–8-cm/3-inch round cutter
   or bowl
piping bag, fitted with
   a star nozzle/tip

SERVES 12–14

Preheat the oven to 180°C (350°F) Gas 4.

Make the 2 quantities of Vanilla Cake and divide between the prepared cake pans. Bake on the middle shelf of the preheated oven for 30–35 minutes, or until a skewer inserted into the middle of the cakes comes out clean. Let the cakes cool in the pans for 10 minutes before turning out on to wire cooling racks. Turn the cakes the right way up and let cool completely.

Level off the tops of the cakes with a sharp knife to make them both the same height. Use the round cutter or small bowl to cut a circle out of the middle of the round cake (you will not need this portion for the finished cake). Imagining the round cake as a clock face, cut out the section that would be 9–12 o'clock and discard.

Trim the edges of the square cake and cut in half to give 2 rectangles, each 10 x 20 cm/ 4 x 8 inches. Cut one of these pieces into a smaller rectangle of roughly 15 x 10 cm/ 6 x 4 inches.

Place the round cake at the bottom of a large board with the cut-out section on the left-hand side. Position the larger rectangle as the upward part of the 5 and the smaller piece as the top.

Tint the buttercream your desired shade of blue with the blue food colouring paste (page 17). Cover the whole cake with two-thirds of the buttercream, spreading evenly with a palette knife. Tint the remaining buttercream a contrasting colour and use to pipe rosettes around the edge of the cake.

This is a fool-proof method for making meringues that are slightly chewy in the middle but still crisp on the outside. For the sake of your arms, make the mixture in an electric freestanding mixer because it takes 10 minutes for the meringue to become really stiff and glossy. The cooked meringues will keep for 3–4 days in an airtight container.

meringue mountain

300 g/1½ cups (caster) sugar
5 large egg whites
pink food colouring paste
blue food colouring paste
edible silver balls and coloured sprinkles
1 tablespoon cocoa

2 solid baking sheets, lined with baking parchment

MAKES 12

Preheat the oven to 200°C (400°F) Gas 6.

Tip the sugar into a small roasting pan and warm in the preheated oven for about 7 minutes, or until hot to the touch. Turn the oven down to 110°C (225°F) Gas ¼.

Meanwhile, whisk the egg whites in an electric freestanding mixer until frothy. Tip all of the hot sugar on to the egg whites in one go and continue to mix on high speed for about 10 minutes until the meringue mixture is very stiff, white and cold.

Divide the mixture between 3 bowls. Add tiny amounts of pink food colouring paste to one bowl using a cocktail stick/toothpick and very

gently fold in using a large metal spoon until the colour has marbled the meringue.

Using 2 tablespoons, dollop the meringue into 4 even-sized mounds on to the prepared baking sheets. Repeat with the blue food colouring paste.

Sift the cocoa into the last bowl of meringue and gently fold in until the meringue is marbled with cocoa.

Sprinkle edible silver balls and coloured sprinkles all over the meringues, then bake in the preheated oven for 1½–1¾ hours. Remove from the oven and let cool on the baking sheets. Pile up on a serving plate.

Everyone loves a cupcake. You can go as pretty or as crazy as you like with the decorations on these little treats. Get the birthday girl to help you decorate.

princess cupcakes

1 quantity Large Basic
   Vanilla Cake (page 11)
1 quantity Buttercream
   (page 14)
food colouring pastes of
   your choice
coloured sprinkles

*piping bags, fitted with star
   nozzles/tips*
*2 x 12-hole muffin pans,
   lined with 18–20 paper
   cupcake cases*

MAKES 18–20

Preheat the oven to 180°C (350°F) Gas 4.

Make the Vanilla Cake and divide between the cupcake cases. Bake on the middle shelf of the preheated oven for 20–25 minutes, or until a skewer inserted into the middle of the cupcakes comes out clean. Let the cupcakes cool in the pans for 10 minutes before turning out on to a wire cooling rack. Turn the cupcakes the right way up and let cool completely.

Divide the buttercream between 3 or 4 bowls, depending how many shades of food colouring you are planning to use. Tint each bowl your desired colour (page 17).

Fill the piping bags with your coloured buttercream and pipe generous swirls of it on top of each cupcake. Decorate with sprinkles and serve on a tiered stand.

Look out for ice cream cone cups that have flat bottoms and will stand upright in the muffin pans while baking. Tint the buttercream pink for strawberry ice cream and scatter with sliced fresh strawberries or a couple of fresh cherries. These cupcakes are best made on the day of the birthday party.

'ice cream' cupcakes

125 g/1 stick unsalted
   butter, room temperature
125 g/1 cup (caster) sugar
2 large eggs, beaten
1 teaspoon vanilla extract
125 g/1 cup plain/all-
   purpose flour
1½ teaspoons baking
   powder
2 tablespoons milk,
   room temperature
10 ice cream cone cups
   (with flat bottoms)
10 flaked chocolate bars

BUTTERCREAM
250 g/2 sticks unsalted
   butter, room temperature
500 g/4 cups icing/
   confectioners' sugar,
   sifted
1 teaspoon vanilla extract

12-hole muffin pan
piping bag, fitted with
   a star nozzle/tip

MAKES 10

Preheat the oven to 180°C (350°F) Gas 4. Stand the ice cream cones in the muffin pan.

Cream the butter and sugar in an electric mixer or with a handheld electric whisk until pale, light and fluffy. Gradually add the eggs, mixing well between each addition and scraping down the bowl with a rubber spatula from time to time. Stir in the vanilla extract.

Sift the flour and baking powder together, then fold into the creamed mixture. Add the milk and stir until smooth. Divide the mixture between the ice cream cones and bake on the middle shelf of the preheated oven for 20–25 minutes until golden and a skewer inserted in the middle of the cupcakes comes out clean. Let the cupcakes cool in the muffin pan for 10 minutes before turning out on to a wire cooling rack to cool completely.

To make the buttercream, cream the butter, sugar and vanilla extract as above. Fill the piping bag with the buttercream and pipe generous swirls of it on top of each cupcake. Finish with a flaked chocolate bar.

43

This is the perfect birthday cake as it can be made 3 days in advance, kept covered in the freezer, then decorated with the chopped mints just before serving.

ice cream layer cake

175 g/ ¾ cup plus 2
   tablespoons caster/
   superfine sugar
3 large egg whites
1 quantity Medium Basic
   Chocolate Cake (page 11)
1 litre/2 pints good-quality
   vanilla ice cream
1.5 litres/3 pints good-
   quality chocolate ice
   cream
200 g/6½ oz. chocolate
   mint matchsticks or
   chocolate bittermints,
   chopped
mint humbugs or similar,
   roughly chopped

*33 x 23 x 6-cm/13 x 9-inch
cake pan, greased and
lined with greased baking
parchment*

SERVES 12

Preheat the oven to 200°C (400°F) Gas 6.

Tip the sugar into a small roasting pan and warm in the preheated oven for about 5 minutes. Turn the oven down to 110°C (225°F) Gas ¼.

Meanwhile, whisk the egg whites in an electric mixer until frothy. Tip all of the hot sugar on to the egg whites in one go and continue to mix on high speed for about 8 minutes until the meringue mixture is very stiff, white and cold.

Spoon into the prepared cake pan, spread level using a palette knife and cook on the middle shelf of the oven for 1½ hours, or until the surface is crisp. Remove from the oven and leave in the pan to cool completely. When cold, remove from the pan and clean the pan, ready for baking the cake layers.

To make the cake layers, grease the cake pan and baseline with greased baking parchment. Preheat the oven to 180°C (350°F) Gas 4.

Make the Chocolate Cake and spoon into the prepared cake pan. Bake on the middle shelf of the preheated oven for 20–25 minutes. Let the cake cool in the pan for 10 minutes before turning out on to a wire cooling rack. Turn the cake the right way up and let cool completely.

To assemble the cake you will need the vanilla ice cream and one-quarter of the chocolate ice cream to be soft so transfer them to the fridge for 20 minutes.

Using a long, serrated knife cut the cake in half to give 2 smaller rectangles roughly 23 x 16 cm/9 x 6½ inches. Carefully remove the baking parchment from the meringue and cut the meringue in the same way.

Tip the vanilla ice cream into a bowl and stir through the chocolate mint matchsticks.

Working quickly, place one cake layer on a board and spread with half the vanilla ice cream. Top with a layer of meringue. Spread the chocolate ice cream over the meringue and cover with the remaining meringue layer. Spread with the remaining vanilla ice cream and the remaining chocolate cake. Cover the cake with clingfilm/plastic wrap and place in the freezer on rapid freeze for at least 2 hours or until solid. Transfer to a serving plate and neaten the edges with a long knife.

Allow the remaining chocolate ice cream to soften slightly in the fridge for 20 minutes, then use to spread all over the top and sides of the cake. Freeze again for about 1 hour.

When you are ready to serve the cake, scatter the top with the mint humbugs.

If you don't like marzipan, you can spread a layer of buttercream over the cake before covering it with the icing. Beware that the cake needs to be left overnight (in an airtight container) to give the icing time to set.

snakes & ladders

1 quantity Extra Large Basic
   Vanilla Cake (page 11)
6 tablespoons apricot or
   raspberry jam
750 g/1½ lbs. marzipan
1 kg/2 lbs. ready-to-roll
   fondant icing
green food colouring paste
yellow food colouring paste
black writing icing
assorted gummy snakes

25.5-cm/10-inch square
   cake pan, greased and
   baselined with greased
   baking parchment
ribbon (optional)

SERVES 15–20

Preheat the oven to 180°C (350°F) Gas 4.

Make the Vanilla Cake and spoon into the prepared cake pan. Bake on the middle shelf of the preheated oven for 40–45 minutes, or until a skewer inserted into the middle of the cake comes out clean. Let the cake cool in the pan for 10 minutes before turning out on to a wire cooling rack. Turn the cake the right way up and let cool completely.

Level off the top of the cake with a sharp knife if necessary. Place the cake on a serving plate.

Heat the jam in a small saucepan until runny, sift, then use to brush the top and sides of the cake.

Lightly dust the work surface with icing/confectioners' sugar and roll the marzipan out to a square slightly larger than the cake. Cover the top and sides of the cake with marzipan, smoothing the surface with sugar-dusted hands and trimming off any excess. Set aside for at least 1 hour.

Lightly brush the marzipan with a little cooled boiled water.

Lightly dust the work surface with more sugar and roll three-quarters of the icing out to a square slightly larger than the cake. Cover the top and sides of the cake with icing, smoothing the surface with sugar-dusted hands and trimming off any excess.

Divide the remaining icing into 2 even portions and tint one half yellow and the other green (page 17). Thinly roll out and cut into even-sized squares to make a chequerboard pattern on top of the cake. Stick in place with a little cooled boiled water. Set aside to dry overnight in an airtight container.

The next day, use the writing icing to draw numbers and ladders on the squares. Tie a ribbon, if using, around the bottom of the cake and decorate with an assortment of gummy snakes.

Bake the cake base the day before you plan to frost these fondant fancies and store in an airtight container overnight – this makes them easier to cut and frost. These little cakes are perfect for just a couple of mouthfuls.

fondant fancies

150 g/1½ sticks unsalted
   butter, room temperature
150 g/¾ cup (caster) sugar
2 large eggs, beaten
150 g/1¼ cups plain/all-
   purpose flour
2 teaspoons baking powder
3–4 tablespoons milk,
   room temperature
50 g/⅓ cup ground almonds
grated zest and juice of
   ½ unwaxed lemon
2 tablespoons lemon curd
1 tablespoon apricot jam
100 g/3½ oz. marzipan
sugar flowers
edible silver balls

ICING
500 g/1 lb. fondant icing sugar
juice of 1 lemon
pink food colouring paste

20-cm/8-inch square cake pan,
   greased and baselined with
   greased baking parchment
piping bag, fitted with
   a small, plain nozzle/tip

MAKES ABOUT 16

Preheat the oven to 180°C (350°F) Gas 4.

Cream the butter and sugar in an electric mixer or with a handheld electric whisk until pale, light and fluffy. Gradually add the eggs, mixing well between each addition and scraping down the bowl with a rubber spatula from time to time.

Sift the flour and baking powder together, then fold half into the creamed mixture followed by half the milk. Add the remaining flour and milk in alternate batches.

Fold in the ground almonds, lemon zest and juice, stir until smooth, then spoon into the prepared cake pan. Bake on the middle shelf of the preheated oven for 25–30 minutes, or until a skewer inserted into the middle of the cake comes out clean. Let the cake cool in the pan for 10 minutes before turning out on to a wire cooling rack. Let cool, then store in an airtight container overnight.

The next day, level off the top of the cake with a sharp knife if necessary. Cut the cake in half horizontally. Place the bottom cake layer on a board and spread the cut surface with the lemon curd. Cover with the other cake layer, cut side down.

Heat the jam in a small saucepan until runny, sift, then use to brush the top of the cake.

Lightly dust the work surface with icing/confectioners' sugar and roll the marzipan out to a square the same size as the cake, using the cake pan as a guide. Lay the marzipan on top of the jam, smoothing the surface with sugar-dusted hands. Trim the sides of the cake, then cut into neat 4-cm/1½-inch cubes.

Mix the fondant icing sugar with lemon juice until it is smooth and thick enough to coat the cakes. Transfer half the icing to a small bowl, add pink food colouring to your desired shade (page 17) and cover with clingfilm/plastic wrap. Colour the remaining icing a different shade of pink. Coat the top and sides of each cake in the 2 colours of fondant icing and let dry on a cooling rack. (The best way to do this is to hold one cake on a fork over the bowl and drizzle the icing over the top and sides to coat evenly.) Cover any leftover icing with clingfilm/plastic wrap. Transfer the cakes to a cooling rack for at least 1 hour or until set.

Fill the piping bag with the remaining fondant icing and pipe thin lines and dots on each cake. Decorate with sugar flowers and edible silver balls. Let dry before serving.

animals

This is my favourite cake and it's so simple. All of the chocolates used in this recipe are easily found in the supermarket or sweet shop/candy store. Look for chocolate buttons in different sizes.

wise owl

1 quantity Extra Large Basic Vanilla or Chocolate Cake (page 11)
1 quantity Chocolate Fudge Frosting (page 15)
chocolate buttons in different sizes
chocolate vermicelli
1 flaked chocolate bar
1 chocolate-covered toffee bar

2 x 23-cm/9-inch round cake pans, greased and baselined with greased baking parchment
piping bag, fitted with a star nozzle/tip

SERVES 12–16

Preheat the oven to 180°C (350°F) Gas 4.

Make the Vanilla Cake mixture and divide between the prepared cake pans. Bake on the middle shelf of the preheated oven for 30–35 minutes, or until a skewer inserted into the middle of the cakes comes out clean. Let the cakes cool in the pans for 10 minutes before turning out on to a wire cooling rack. Turn the cakes the right way up and let cool completely.

Level off the tops of the cakes with a sharp knife if necessary. Place one cake on a serving plate and spread the cut surface with about 3 tablespoons of the Chocolate Fudge Frosting. Cover with the other cake layer, cut side down. Cover the top and sides of the whole cake with three-quarters of the remaining Chocolate Fudge Frosting, spreading evenly with a palette knife.

Arrange the chocolate buttons over the bottom half of the cake to resemble feathers and cover the top half of the cake with chocolate vermicelli. Fill the piping bag with the remaining Chocolate Frosting and use this to pipe feathers around the owl's face.

Position assorted chocolate buttons on top of the sprinkles for the eyes. Cut the flaked chocolate bar into thin pieces and push into the bottom edge of the cake to make legs. Cut the toffee bar in half. Slice one half diagonally into 2 pieces for the wings and push one into each side of the owl. Cut the remaining toffee bar at an angle to make a beak and position on the owl's face.

I have covered this rabbit in meringue frosting but you could use buttercream coloured to your desired shade. For the bunny's tail you only need one cupcake, so freeze the leftovers or turn them into flowers, like those on page 122, and place them around the bunny.

bunny rabbit

1 quantity Extra Large Basic Vanilla Cake (page 11)
1 quantity Small Basic Vanilla Cake (page 11)
1 quantity Meringue Frosting (page 15)
pink food colouring paste
2 jelly beans or brown sugar-coated chocolate drops
black writing icing

33 x 23 x 6-cm/13 x 9-inch cake pan, greased and baselined with greased baking parchment
6-hole muffin pan, lined with paper cases

SERVES 12

Preheat the oven to 180°C (350°F) Gas 4.

Make the Vanilla Cake mixtures (separately) and spoon the Extra Large into the prepared cake pan and divide the Small between the paper cases. Bake on the middle shelf of the preheated oven until a skewer inserted into the middle of the cakes comes out clean – 40 minutes for the cake and 20–25 minutes for the cupcakes. Let the cakes cool in the pan for 10 minutes before turning out on to wire cooling racks. Turn the cakes the right way up and let cool completely.

Refer to the diagrams on page 20 and use to draw a similar rabbit shape on a piece of paper. Cut out and lay on top of the cake. Cut around with a sharp knife and use the trimmings to make the head and ears. Arrange the body parts on a large platter.

Take 3–4 tablespoons of the Meringue Frosting for the ears and tail and set aside in a small bowl. Completely cover the top and sides of the rabbit with the Meringue Frosting, peaking the meringue with the back of a spoon so that it looks like fur.

Stir a tiny amount of pink food colouring paste (page 17) into the reserved frosting to make a pale pink. Peel the paper case off one cupcake and cover the cupcake in pink frosting. Fill in the insides of the ears with pink frosting too. Arrange the cupcake on top of the rabbit for the tail.

Position the jelly beans or chocolate drops on the rabbit's face to make an eye and the nose. Using the writing icing, draw whiskers on the face. Set aside for about 1 hour to set slightly before serving.

This cake will appeal to a younger child. Make the cake in advance and assemble on the day of the party. To make the ears and nose you will need to make a batch of cupcakes but since you only need a small number of them for the teddy bear cake, the remaining cupcakes can either be frozen for another time or covered with frosting and served alongside the teddy.

teddy bear

1 quantity Large Basic
   Vanilla or Chocolate Cake
   (page 11)
1 quantity Small Basic
   Vanilla or Chocolate Cake
   (page 11)
1 quantity Chocolate Fudge
   Frosting (page 15)
assorted chocolate drops
   and buttons
ribbon

*2 x 20-cm/8-inch round
   cake pans, greased and
   baselined with greased
   baking parchment*
*12-hole muffin pan, lined
   with 6 paper cases and 1
   mini paper cupcake case*

SERVES 10

Preheat the oven to 180°C (350°F) Gas 4.

Make the Vanilla Cake mixtures (separately) and spoon the Large into the prepared cake pans and divide the Small one between the paper cases. Bake on the middle shelf of the preheated oven until a skewer inserted into the middle of the cakes comes out clean – 30 minutes for the cakes, 25 minutes for the cupcakes and 15 minutes for the mini cupcake. Let all the cakes cool in the pans for 10 minutes before turning out on to wire cooling racks. Turn the cakes the right way up and let cool completely.

Use a long, serrated knife to level the tops of the cakes if necessary. Place one cake on a serving plate and spread 3–4 tablespoons of Chocolate Frosting over the top. Top with the second cake. Use three-quarters of the remaining Chocolate Frosting to cover the top and sides of the whole cake, spreading evenly with a palette knife.

Peel the paper case off one cupcake and cut the cupcake in half horizontally. Position one half on each side of the head to make the ears. Cover the tops of 2 other cupcakes with frosting and place on top of the halved cupcakes so that they are roughly level with the top of the teddy's face.

Peel the paper case off the mini cupcake and completely cover the cupcake with frosting. Position in the middle of the cake to make the teddy's nose. Arrange the chocolate drops on the face for the eyes, mouth and ears. Make a bow out of the ribbon and place at the teddy's neck.

These funny cupcakes look tricky but are actually very simple to make. The only fancy equipment you'll need are a couple of piping bags, nozzles/tips and a steady hand. The cupcakes can be made ahead and stored, undecorated, in the freezer in plastic containers.

animal face cupcakes

1 quantity Large Basic Vanilla Cake (page 11)
1 quantity Buttercream (page 14)
brown food colouring paste
black food colouring paste
2 small liquorice sweets
12 sugar-coated chocolate drops
black writing icing

3 piping bags, fitted with star nozzles/tips
12-hole muffin pan, lined with paper cupcake cases
12-hole mini cupcake pan, lined with mini paper cupcake cases

MAKES 12

Preheat the oven to 180°C (350°F) Gas 4.

Make the Vanilla Cake mixture and use to fill each cupcake case with a big tablespoon, and the mini cases with a big teaspoonful. Bake on the middle shelf of the preheated oven – the cupcakes will take 20–25 minutes and the mini cupcakes will take 10–15 minutes. A skewer inserted into the middle of the cakes should come out clean. Let cool in the pans for 10 minutes, then transfer to a wire rack to cool completely.

Divide the buttercream between 3 bowls and tint one brown and one grey with the brown and black food colouring pastes (page 17) and leave the third plain.

Fill the piping bags with the coloured buttercreams. Pipe lines of buttercream on top of the cupcakes, from the outside to the middle in a slight dome – cover 4 of the cupcakes with brown buttercream, 4 with grey, and 4 with white. Repeat with the mini cupcakes, making ears at the top of each cake.

Cut the liquorice into tiny pieces for noses and position one on each mini cupcake. Cut the chocolate drops in half and position on the ears. Using the black writing icing, pipe eyes and whiskers onto each mini cupcake. Position the mini cakes at an angle on top of the cupcakes and push gently until they are firmly stuck in place.

This is guaranteed to appeal to the dinosaur-loving birthday boy or girl. Look out for chocolate-coated wafers in the cookie aisle of the supermarket as they make ideal spines. Garnish the serving plate with chocolate-coated 'boulders'.

jolly green dinosaur

1 quantity Extra Large Basic
   Vanilla Cake (page 11)
1 quantity Buttercream
   (page 14)
green food colouring paste
brown food colouring paste
14 mini chocolate drops
chocolate-coated wafers
green diamond-shaped
   candies
chocolate sprinkles
green sprinkles
2 white chocolate buttons
black writing icing

2 x 23-cm/9-inch round
   cake pans, greased and
   baselined with greased
   baking parchment
piping bag, fitted with
   a star nozzle/tip

SERVES 10–12

Preheat the oven to 180°C (350°F) Gas 4.

Make the Vanilla Cake mixture and divide between the prepared cake pans. Bake on the middle shelf of the preheated oven for 35–40 minutes, or until a skewer inserted into the middle of the cakes comes out clean. Let the cakes cool in the pans for 10 minutes before turning out on to wire cooling racks. Let cool completely, then store overnight in an airtight container.

The next day, assemble the dinosaur (refer to the diagrams on page 20). Use a long, serrated knife to level the tops of the cakes if necessary. Lay the cakes one on top of the other, cut sides facing each other. Cut the bottom third off both cakes and reserve. Separate the cakes again and spread some of the buttercream over one cut side. Sandwich the 2 cakes together, then place upright (resting on the flat side) in the middle of a serving plate.

The reserved pieces of cake should look like orange segments. Take one segment and cut it in half to make 2 rough triangle shapes. Sandwich the 2 shapes together with a little

buttercream and position upright as the head of the dinosaur. Cut 4 strips from the straight side of the remaining segment and stick 2 strips with buttercream on each side of the dinosaur to make each leg. You should have a slim segment shape leftover. Cut this in half to make 2 rough triangle shapes. Sandwich the 2 shapes together with a little buttercream and position upright as the tail.

Reserve 4 tablespoons of the buttercream in a small bowl. Tint the remaining buttercream green with the green food colouring paste (page 17). Fill a piping bag with the green buttercream and use to cover the dinosaur with rosettes. Tint the reserved buttercream brown and pipe little feet on to the legs. Press on the mini chocolate buttons for the claws.

Push the chocolate-coated wafers all down the back of the dinosaur to make scales and position the green diamond candies between the wafers. Scatter the chocolate and green sprinkles all over the dinosaur. Stick the white chocolate buttons on the face for the eyes and use the black writing icing for the centre of the eyes and to make a mouth. Position the last mini chocolate buttons as nostrils.

For this recipe you need only one cupcake, but if you make a batch, the remaining cupcakes can either be frozen for use another time or frosted and served alongside the hedgehog. You could even buy extra matchsticks and make the cupcakes into baby hedgehogs!

prickly hedgehog

1 quantity Large Basic
   Vanilla or Chocolate Cake
   (page 11)
1 quantity Small Basic
   Vanilla or Chocolate Cake
   (page 11)
1 quantity Chocolate Fudge
   Frosting (page 15)
chocolate vermicelli
about 500 g/1 lb. chocolate
   mint matchsticks
3 chocolate drops

*2-litre/quart ovenproof
   glass bowl, greased and
   dusted with flour*
*6-hole muffin pan, lined
   with paper cases*

SERVES 10

Preheat the oven to 180°C (350°F) Gas 4.

Make the Vanilla Cake mixtures (separately) and spoon the Large into the prepared bowl and divide the Small between the paper cases. Bake on the middle shelf of the preheated oven until a skewer inserted into the middle of the cakes comes out clean – 1 hour for the cake and 20–25 minutes for the cupcakes. Let the cakes cool in the bowl or pan for 10 minutes before turning out on to wire cooling racks to cool completely.

Use a long, serrated knife to level the bottom of the cake if necessary. Cut the cake into 3 even horizontal layers. Sandwich the cake together with 3 tablespoons of Chocolate Fudge Frosting between each layer.

Place the cake on a serving plate and cover it with Chocolate Frosting, spreading evenly with a palette knife.

Peel the paper case off one cupcake and level off the domed top. Turn upside down and cover the top and sides with frosting. Scatter with the chocolate vermicelli and position on the plate next to the larger cake for the head.

To make the spines, cut the matchsticks in half and push them into the body of the hedgehog until it is totally covered. Push the chocolate drops into the head for eyes.

This is a very simple cake to make and assemble and can be easily baked on the day of the party. You only need one cupcake so freeze the rest for another time.

fluffy sheep

1 quantity Large Basic
    Vanilla Cake (page 11)
1 quantity Small Basic
    Vanilla Cake (page 11)
1 quantity Buttercream
    (page 14)
600 g/1 lb. 4 oz. white mini
    marshmallows
2 pink regular
    marshmallows
chocolate vermicelli
2 chocolate drops
black writing icing

*2-litre/quart ovenproof
    glass bowl, greased and
    dusted with flour*
*6-hole muffin pan, lined
    with paper cases*
4 cocktail sticks/toothpicks

SERVES ABOUT 10

Preheat the oven to 180°C (350°F) Gas 4.

Make the Vanilla Cake mixtures (separately) and spoon the Large into the prepared bowl and divide the Small between the paper cases. Bake on the middle shelf of the preheated oven until a skewer inserted into the middle of the cake comes out clean – 1 hour for the cake and 20–25 minutes for the cupcakes. Let the cakes cool in the bowl or pan for 10 minutes before turning out on to wire cooling racks to cool completely.

Use a long, serrated knife to level the bottom of the cake if necessary. Put the cake, flat side down, on a serving plate and cover it with buttercream, spreading evenly with a palette knife.

Peel the paper case off one cupcake (and freeze the rest of the cupcakes). Cover the cupcake with buttercream, position on top of the sheep for the head and secure in place with a cocktail stick/toothpick.

Cover the body and the head of the sheep with the mini marshmallows, leaving a space for the sheep's face. Carefully coat a regular marshmallow with buttercream and stick to the face. Secure with a cocktail stick/toothpick.

Cover the face and nose with chocolate vermicelli and press to stick.

Cut the remaining regular marshmallow in half, pinch the ends together to make ear shapes and attach to the sides of the head with cocktail sticks/toothpicks.

Using the black writing icing, pipe a nose and mouth on the face and use to attach chocolate drop eyes.

The cake quantity used in this recipe is enough to make the body and head of the dog and 8 mini cupcakes. You will only need one cupcake for the finished dog and the remaining cupcakes can be frozen for another time.

mungo the dog

1 quantity Large Basic
  Vanilla Cake (page 11)
200 g/6½ oz. desiccated
  coconut
4 plain, storebought mini
  Swiss cake rolls
1 quantity Buttercream
  (page 14)
red food colouring paste
edible silver balls
12 mini chocolate drops
2 white chocolate buttons
black writing icing
2 chocolate-coated wafers

1.2-litre/5-cup and 275-ml/
  1¼-cup ovenproof
  pudding bowls, greased
  and dusted with flour
12-hole mini cupcake pan,
  lined with 8 mini paper
  cupcake cases
cocktail sticks/toothpicks
piping bag, fitted with
  a star nozzle/tip

SERVES 12

Preheat the oven to 180°C (350°F) Gas 4.

Make the Vanilla Cake mixture and spoon into the prepared bowls until they are two-thirds full. Use the remaining mixture to fill the cupcakes cases, allowing roughly 1½–2 teaspoons of mixture per cupcake. Bake all the cakes in the middle of the preheated oven until a skewer inserted into the middle of the cakes comes out clean – 10–15 minutes for the mini cupcakes, 30 minutes for the smaller bowl and 40–45 minutes for the larger one. Let the cakes cool in the bowls or pan for 10 minutes before turning out on to wire cooling racks to cool.

Put the desiccated coconut in a dry frying pan and toast until lightly golden, tossing frequently to stop it burning. Set aside to cool while you start on the cake.

Use a long, serrated knife to level the tops of the cakes if necessary. Put the larger one, flat side down, on a large plate.

Take the smaller cake and put it, cut side down, on a board. Trim a little off 2 sides to make a muzzle shape. Arrange the head

on top of the body, flat side down, and slightly forwards. Secure with cocktail sticks/toothpicks.

Peel the paper case off the mini cupcake and attach the cupcake to the muzzle with cocktail sticks/toothpicks. Arrange the mini rolls, (2 upright in the front and 2 flat at the back) to make the legs.

Reserve 3–4 tablespoons of the buttercream in a small bowl. Cover the dog with the remaining buttercream, spreading evenly with a palette knife. Scatter the toasted coconut over the buttercream and press lightly to stick.

Tint the reserved buttercream red with the red food colouring paste (page 17) and use to fill the piping bag. Pipe rosettes around the neck of the dog to make a collar and decorate with silver balls.

Use the mini chocolate drops for the claws and white chocolate buttons for the eyes. Pipe a nose and mouth on the head using black writing icing. Finally, push the chocolate-coated wafers into the top of the head for the ears.

This is the perfect cake for the novice baker as it only requires two round cake pans and no tricky assembly or frosting. It probably appeals more to a younger child. You could also use brown or black colouring to make a tabby or grey cat instead of the ginger cat here, or you can frost the cake with Chocolate Fudge Frosting (page 15).

marmalade cat

1 quantity Medium Basic Vanilla Cake (page 11)

1 quantity Large Basic Vanilla Cake (page 11)

1 quantity Buttercream (page 14)

orange food colouring paste

2 green fruit pastilles or similar

1 small liquorice candy

1 long liquorice shoelace

black writing icing

18-cm/7-inch and 23-cm/ 9-inch round cake pans, greased and baselined with greased baking parchment

SERVES 12–14

Preheat the oven to 180°C (350°F) Gas 4.

Make the Vanilla Cake mixtures (separately) and spoon the Medium quantity into the smaller pan and the Large quantity into the larger pan. Bake on the middle shelf of the preheated oven until a skewer inserted into the middle of the cakes comes out clean – about 30 minutes for the smaller pan and 35–40 minutes for the larger pan. Let the cakes cool in the pans for 10 minutes before turning out on to wire cooling racks.

Reserve 4–5 tablespoons of the buttercream in a small bowl. Tint the remaining buttercream orange with the orange food colouring paste (page 17).

Use a long, serrated knife to level the tops of the cakes and make them the same height.

Cut about one-third off the top of the larger cake in a leaf shape (refer to the diagrams on page 20). Fit the smaller cake into the space. Cut the leaf shape in half to make 2 triangles and position at the top of the smaller cake to make the ears.

Cover the cat with the orange buttercream, spreading evenly with a palette knife. Carefully spread the reserved plain buttercream to make a tummy shape and the insides of the ears.

Position the fruit pastilles on the cat's face for the eyes. Slice the liquorice candy into thin slices to make the nose and position the liquorice shoelace as the tail and the mouth. Use the black writing icing to make the whiskers and the pupils in the eyes.

Look out for a suitable elephant picture that will work well as a template for this cake, or just use the picture here. Photocopy and enlarge the picture to the same size as the cake and cut out to use as a template. Make the cake the day before you plan to decorate it. Once completely cold, wrap up and refrigerate overnight. This will make cutting out the shape easier. For more tips on using templates and cutting a cake base, see pages 18–19.

indian elephant

1 quantity Extra Large Basic
    Vanilla Cake (page 11)
1 quantity Buttercream
    (page 14)
black food colouring paste
red food colouring paste
black writing icing
white writing icing
red writing icing
yellow writing icing
edible silver and coloured
    balls
coloured candy

33 x 23 x 6-cm/13 x
    9-inch cake pan, greased
    and baselined with
    greased baking
    parchment
piping bag, fitted with
    a star nozzle/tip

SERVES 12

Preheat the oven to 180°C (350°F) Gas 4.

Make the Vanilla Cake mixture and spoon into the prepared cake pan. Bake on the middle shelf of the preheated oven for 40 minutes, or until a skewer inserted into the middle of the cake comes out clean. Let the cake to cool in the pan for 10 minutes before turning out on to a wire cooling rack. Turn the cake the right way up and let cool completely. If you have time, wrap the cold cake in clingfilm/plastic wrap and refrigerate overnight before continuing.

When you are ready to assemble the cake, draw an elephant shape on a sheet of paper the same size as the cake, lay on top of the cake and using a small, sharp knife carefully cut around the paper template. Use the leftover bits of cake for a trifle, in lunchboxes or to snack on.

Reserve one-quarter of the buttercream and set aside. Tint the remaining buttercream grey with the black food colouring paste (page 17). Cover the elephant with the buttercream, spreading evenly with a palette knife.

Put 3–4 tablespoons of the reserved buttercream in a small bowl and tint red with the red food colouring paste. Fill the piping bag with the buttercream and use to pipe rosettes in the shape of a cap on the elephant's head.

Use the remaining plain buttercream to make a leaf-shaped saddle on the elephant's back. Use the different writing icings to pipe decorative lines over the legs, trunk and neck, and as tassels below the saddle. Use the white writing icing to fill in the tusk. Decorate the elephant with edible silver and coloured balls and use the candy to trim the saddle.

transport

You could frost this cake using Chocolate Fudge Frosting from page 15 instead of the black buttercream if you like. Look out for Jolly Roger images to cut out and secure to wooden skewers for decoration.

pirate ship

1 quantity Extra Large Basic
   Vanilla Cake (page 11)
1 quantity Buttercream
   (page 14)
black food colouring paste
2 latticed chocolate bars
   or similar
red writing icing
yellow writing icing
sugar-coated chocolate
   drops
chequered liquorice candy
   or similar
25 g/2 oz. dark/semisweet
   chocolate, chopped

33 x 23 x 6-cm/13 x 9-inch
   cake pan, greased and
   baselined with greased
   baking parchment
Jolly Roger pictures
   in various sizes
3 or 4 wooden skewers
glue

SERVES 12–14

Preheat the oven to 180°C (350°F) Gas 4.

Make the Vanilla Cake mixture and spoon into the prepared cake pan. Bake on the middle shelf of the preheated oven for 45 minutes, or until a skewer inserted into the middle of the cake comes out clean. Let the cake cool in the pan for 10 minutes before turning out on to a wire cooling rack. Turn the cake the right way up and let cool completely.

Use a long, serrated knife to level the top of the cake if necessary.

Refer to pages 18–19 for step-by-step instructions on cutting and assembling the cake. Sandwich the pieces together with a little buttercream.

Tint the remaining buttercream black with the black food colouring paste (page 17) and use to cover the whole cake, spreading evenly with a palette knife.

Measure the gap along the side of the ship and cut the latticed chocolate bars to fit. Press them into the cake slightly so that they stick to the buttercream, making railings.

Decorate the pirate ship with the red and yellow writing icing, as desired. Stick chocolate drops on to the prow of the ship. Cut the chequered liquorice candy in slices and position as windows on the side.

To make the gangplank, melt the dark chocolate in a heatproof bowl set over a pan of barely simmering water (do not let the base of the bowl touch the water). Stir until melted and smooth. Spread into a rough rectangle shape on a piece of baking parchment, chill until set (20–30 minutes), then cut into a neat plank shape with a hot knife. Push gently into the side of the ship.

Stick Jolly Roger flags on either side of wooden skewers and push them into the ship.

I have made this a pink fifties-type car but if your child has a favourite car from a story book, use an image from it as a template and tint the buttercream accordingly.

fifties-style car

1 quantity Extra Large Basic
   Vanilla Cake (page 11)
1 quantity Buttercream
   (page 14)
pink food colouring paste
red liquorice shoelace
   or similar
black writing icing
silver writing icing
2 white chocolate rainbow
   buttons or similar
edible silver balls
red writing icing
pink tube-shaped candy

*33 x 23 x 6-cm/13 x 9-inch
   cake pan, greased and
   baselined with greased
   baking parchment*

SERVES 12

Preheat the oven to 180°C (350°F) Gas 4.

Make the Vanilla Cake mixture and spoon into the prepared cake pan. Bake on the middle shelf of the preheated oven for 45 minutes, or until a skewer inserted into the middle of the cake comes out clean. Let the cake cool in the pan for 10 minutes before turning out on to a wire cooling rack. Turn the cake the right way up and let cool completely.

Level off the top of the cake with a sharp knife if necessary. Cut out a paper template in the shape of a car, lay on top of the cake and using a small, sharp knife carefully cut around the template. Use the trimmings for a trifle, in lunchboxes or to snack on.

Set aside 2–3 tablespoons of the buttercream in a small bowl. Tint the remaining buttercream pink with the pink food colouring paste (page 17) and use to cover the cake, spreading evenly with a palette knife.

Press the red liquorice shoelace across the car and trim off the excess with a sharp knife. Use the black and silver writing icing to draw the outlines of the doors, windows and wheels. Spread the reserved buttercream into circles

for the wheels, adding the rainbow drops and edible silver balls for hubcaps.

Use the red writing icing to outline the car and trim the liquorice shoelace. Add edible silver balls for door handles and headlights. Write the child's name on the car with writing icing. Stick the pink tube-shaped candy in the back for the exhaust.

You can decorate this balloon simply in one or two colours or be as imaginative as you like.

hot air balloon

1 quantity Extra Large Basic Vanilla Cake (page 11)
1 quantity Buttercream (page 14)
brown food colouring paste
red food colouring paste
green food colouring paste
blue food colouring paste
yellow food colouring paste
purple food colouring paste
black writing icing
8 chocolate matchsticks, about 5 cm/2 inches long

33 x 23 x 6-cm/13 x 9-inch cake pan, greased and baselined with greased baking parchment

SERVES 12

Preheat the oven to 180°C (350°F) Gas 4.

Make the Vanilla Cake mixture and spoon into the prepared cake pan. Bake on the middle shelf of the preheated oven for 45 minutes, or until a skewer inserted into the middle of the cake comes out clean. Let the cake cool in the pan for 10 minutes before turning out on to a wire cooling rack. Turn the cake the right way up and let cool completely.

Put 3–4 tablespoons of the buttercream in a bowl and tint it brown with the brown food colouring paste (page 17). Divide the remaining buttercream between 5 bowls and tint each one a different colour.

Refer to the diagrams on page 21 and use to draw a similar balloon shape on a piece of paper. Make it as large as will fit on the baked cake. Cut out the template and lay it on top of the cake, then cut around it with a sharp knife. You should have 2 good corners of the cake left – cut these off in equal triangles (see diagram) and stick together with a little buttercream to make a square basket shape. Position the balloon on a large plate and spread the coloured buttercreams in stripes over the balloon using a narrow knife. Pipe lines between the stripes with black writing icing. Cover the underside of the balloon with brown buttercream. Push the chocolate matchsticks into the underside of the balloon.

Position the basket below the balloon and cover with brown buttercream, making a weave effect with a fork. Push against the matchsticks carefully.

Choose this cake for your child's party and you can complete the theme by putting plastic farm animals around the tractor!

big green tractor

1 quantity Extra Large Basic Vanilla Cake (page 11)
1 quantity Small Basic Vanilla Cake (page 11)
1 quantity Buttercream (page 14)
green food colouring paste
4 tablespoons raspberry or apricot jam
black food colouring paste
4 round yellow fruit candies
liquorice twist or similar
black writing icing
yellow writing icing
4 yellow sugar-coated chocolate drops
chocolate sprinkles

33 x 23 x 6-cm/13 x 9-inch cake pan, greased and baselined with greased baking parchment
6-hole muffin pan, lined with 4 paper cases and 2 mini paper cupcake cases
piping bag, fitted with a star nozzle/tip

SERVES 12–14

Preheat the oven to 180°C (350°F) Gas 4.

Make the Vanilla Cake mixtures (separately) and spoon the Extra Large into the prepared cake pan and divide the Small between the paper cases. Bake on the middle shelf of the preheated oven until a skewer inserted into the middle of the cakes comes out clean – 45 minutes for the cake and 20–25 minutes for the cupcakes. Let the cakes cool in the pan for 10 minutes before turning out on to a wire cooling rack. Turn the cakes the right way up and let cool completely.

Level off the top of the cake with a sharp knife if necessary. Refer to the diagrams on page 21. Using a long, serrated knife cut the cake in half to give 2 smaller rectangles roughly 33 x 11 cm/13 x 4½ inches. Lay the 2 pieces one on top of the other and cut a square from the end (through both pieces) measuring roughly 11 x 11 cm/4½ x 4½ inches.

Reserve one-quarter of the buttercream in a small bowl. Tint the remainder green with the green food colouring paste (page 17).

Place one large rectangle cake on a serving plate and spread 2 tablespoons of the jam

over the top. Top with the second large rectangle. Sandwich the 2 small squares with another tablespoon of jam and position at one end of the large cake, sticking in place with the last of the jam. Using a long, serrated knife trim the windscreen so that it slopes slightly outward. Cover the whole cake with green buttercream, spreading smoothly.

Tint the reserved buttercream black with the black food colouring paste. Spread a little carefully over the sides and front of the tractor to make windows and a windscreen.

Peel the paper cases off the cupcakes. Cut the top of the cupcakes to make them level and position the mini cupcakes at the front and the regular at the back. Fill the piping bag with the remaining black buttercream and use to pipe lines over the wheels from the outside to the centre. Stick a yellow fruit candy in the middle for a hubcap. Stick the liquorice twist in the bonnet as the exhaust. Use the writing icings to decorate the tractor. Add the yellow chocolate drops as headlights.

Scatter the chocolate sprinkles around the tractor to look like mud.

It can be quite time-consuming making these little trains so unless you have time and patience it would be best to reserve these for a maximum of ten party guests. Make the cake the day before you want to assemble the trains and once cooled, store in the fridge wrapped in clingfilm/plastic wrap overnight. This makes cutting, assembly and frosting easier.

steam train set

1 quantity Large Basic
  Vanilla Cake (page 11)
about 10 tablespoons
  raspberry or apricot jam
10 plain storebought mini
  Swiss cake rolls
1 quantity Buttercream
  (page 14)
red food colouring paste
green food colouring paste
blue food colouring paste
black writing icing
sugar-coated chocolate
  drops
wheel-shaped and tube-
  shaped candies

33 x 23 x 6-cm/13 x 9-inch
cake pan, greased and
baselined with greased
baking parchment

MAKES 10

Preheat the oven to 180°C (350°F) Gas 4.

Make the Vanilla Cake mixture and spoon into the prepared cake pan. Bake on the middle shelf of the preheated oven for 25–30 minutes, or until a skewer inserted into the middle of the cake comes out clean. Let the cake cool in the pan for 10 minutes before turning out on to a wire cooling rack. Turn the cake the right way up and let cool completely.

If necessary, use a long, sharp knife to level off the top of the cake and trim the sides to make them straight.

Put the cake on a board and cut it into strips across the short side (refer to the diagrams on page 21). Each strip should be 4 cm/1⅝ inches wide, so you should get 7 strips out of the cake. Then cut each strip into 3 rectangles. This will give you 21 rectangles each measuring 7 x 4 cm/2¾ x 1⅝ inches.

Place one of the rectangles on the work surface and spread a tablespoon of jam across the top and over one end. Stand another rectangle upright at the jam end and press together. Place a mini cake roll on the top of the rectangle on top of the jam to make the engine. Repeat with the other cake pieces to make 10 trains. You will have 1 rectangle left over to snack on!

Divide the buttercream between 3 bowls and tint each bowl a different colour with the food colouring pastes (page 17). Cover each train with buttercream, spreading evenly with a small palette knife. Use the writing icing to decorate the trains, draw in the windows and write the name of each child on the engine.

Stick chocolate drops and wheel-shaped candies to the sides for the lights and wheels, and push the tube-shaped candy on top of the engine for the chimney stack.

This cake can be baked the day before and frosted on the day of the party. However, the ladder should be kept frozen and added just before serving so that it remains upright.

fire engine

1 quantity Extra Large Basic Vanilla Cake (page 11)
1 quantity Buttercream (page 14)
red food colouring paste
3 tablespoons raspberry or apricot jam
4 liquorice wheels
round and square liquorice candies
black writing icing
yellow writing icing
sugar-coated chocolate drops
blue food colouring paste
yellow food colouring paste
100 g/3½ oz. ready-to-roll fondant icing or sugar paste
1 latticed chocolate bar or similar, frozen

33 x 23 x 6-cm/13 x 9-inch cake pan, greased and baselined with greased baking parchment
piping bag, fitted with a small, plain nozzle/tip

SERVES 12–14

Preheat the oven to 180°C (350°F) Gas 4.

Make the Vanilla Cake mixture and spoon into the prepared cake pan. Bake on the middle shelf of the preheated oven for 45 minutes, or until a skewer inserted into the middle of the cake comes out clean. Let the cake cool in the pan for 10 minutes before turning out on to a wire cooling rack. Turn the cake the right way up and let cool completely.

If necessary, use a long, sharp knife to level off the top of the cake and trim the sides to make them straight.

Using a long, serrated knife cut the cake in half to give 2 smaller rectangles roughly 33 x 11 cm/13 x 4½ inches (refer to the diagrams on page 20). Lay the 2 pieces one on top of the other and cut a rectangle from the end (through both pieces) measuring roughly 9 x 11 cm/3½ x 4½ inches. You will only need one small rectangle so you can pop the second one in a lunchbox!

Reserve 2 tablespoons of the buttercream in a small bowl. Tint the remainder a vibrant red with the red food colouring paste (page 17).

Place one large rectangle cake on a serving plate and spread 2 tablespoons of the jam over the top. Top with the second large rectangle. Spread a tablespoon of jam over the small rectangle and position at one end of the large cake.

Cover the whole cake with red buttercream, spreading evenly with a palette knife. Position 2 liquorice wheels on either side of the cake and the other liquorice candies as the ladder platform and flashing lights on top of the cab. Use the black and yellow writing icings to draw windows. Position the chocolate drops on the front as headlights.

Tint the reserved buttercream blue with the blue food colouring paste and use to fill the piping bag. Pipe lines around the wheels and across the front of the cab.

Lightly dust a clean work surface with icing/confectioners' sugar and knead the fondant icing until pliable. Add yellow food colouring paste and roll between your hands into a hose. Lay the hose at the back of the fire engine and coil around to the front. Push the frozen latticed chocolate bar into the top of the cake just before serving.

You can use Meringue Frosting (page 15) or Buttercream (page 14) for this rocket ship but as the Meringue Frosting is bright white, the finished result is more dramatic. Sparkler candles will make the rocket go off with a blast!

rocket ship

1 quantity Extra Large Basic
  Vanilla Cake (page 11)
1 quantity Meringue
  Frosting (page 15) or
  Buttercream (page 14)
red writing icing
blue and red sugar-coated
  chocolate drops
edible silver balls
'flying saucer' sherbert
  candies
rainbow puffed rice candies

*33 x 23 x 6-cm/13 x 9-inch
  cake pan, greased and
  baselined with greased
  baking parchment*
silver candles

SERVES 12–14

Preheat the oven to 180°C (350°F) Gas 4.

Make the Vanilla Cake mixture and spoon into the prepared cake pan. Bake on the middle shelf of the preheated oven for 45 minutes, or until a skewer inserted into the middle of the cake comes out clean. Let the cake cool in the pan for 10 minutes before turning out on to a wire cooling rack. Turn the cake the right way up and let cool completely.

Level off the top of the cake with a sharp knife if necessary. Place on a large serving plate.

Refer to the diagrams on page 21 and use to draw a similar rocket shape on a piece of paper. Make it as large as will fit on the baked cake. Cut out the template and lay it on top of the cake, then cut around it with a sharp

knife. You should have 2 good corners of the cake left to use as jets – position these upside down on either side of the rocket, at the base.

Working quickly, spread the Meringue Frosting over the top and sides of the rocket, spreading evenly with palette knife. Use a little of the frosting to glue the jets into place.

Use the red writing icing to decorate the rocket and write the child's name up the side, if you like. Decorate with chocolate drops and silver balls. Set aside for 30 minutes for the meringue to harden slightly.

Push the candles into the base of the rocket. Scatter 'flying saucer' candies and rainbow puffed rice around the cake as space debris. Light the candles carefully and serve.

fantasy

I have covered dowelling in pretty ribbons for the carousel but you could also use sticks of rock. To support the top of the carousel you will need the cardboard tube from a roll of foil or similar, and a foil-covered cake board slightly smaller than 20 cm/8 inches in diameter.

magical carousel

1 quantity Extra Large Basic Vanilla Cake (page 11)
1 quantity Glacé Icing (page 15)
1 quantity Gingerbread Shapes (page 12) or Shortbread (page 13), baked into horse shapes
sparkly writing icing
black writing icing
1 quantity Buttercream (page 14)
pink food colouring paste
lilac food colouring paste
edible metallic balls
1 mini sugar-coated chocolate egg
sugar flowers

20-cm/8-inch and 23-cm/9-inch round cake pans, greased and baselined with greased baking parchment
assorted ribbons
6 x 20-cm/8-inch dowelling rods
20-cm/8-inch cardboard tube
2 piping bags, fitted with star nozzles/tips
foil-covered cake board

SERVES 12–14

Preheat the oven to 180°C (350°F) Gas 4.

Make the Vanilla Cake mixture and divide between the prepared cake pans. Bake on the middle shelf of the preheated oven until a skewer inserted into the middle of the cakes comes out clean – 30–35 minutes for the smaller pan and 40 minutes for the larger one. Let the cakes cool in the pans for 10 minutes before turning out on to wire cooling racks.

Meanwhile, spread Glacé Icing over the horse shapes with the back of a spoon. Let set for at least 2 hours. Use sparkly writing icing to decorate the horses and the black writing icing to draw bridles and eyes on the horses' faces. Let dry for a further hour.

Wrap a ribbon around each dowelling rod and the cardboard tube and secure the ends with sticky tape.

When you are ready to assemble the carousel, put the larger cake on a serving plate. Use a long, serrated knife to level the top of the cake if necessary. Spread just less than half the buttercream over the top and sides of the cake, spreading evenly with a palette knife.

Divide the remaining buttercream between 2 bowls and tint them pink and blue with the food colouring pastes (page 17). Fill the piping bags with the buttercream.

Place the second cake on a foil-covered cake board that is slightly smaller than the cake. Pipe buttercream rosettes in coloured sections over the top and sides of the cake and scatter with assorted edible balls. Use more of the sparkly writing icing to pipe lines between the coloured sections. Finish with a mini sugar-coated egg in the middle.

Stick sugar flowers along the bottom cake and finish by piping little rosettes along the bottom and decorating with more edible metallic balls.

Push the ribbon-covered cardboard tube into the middle of the bottom cake all the way down to the plate. Arrange the dowelling around the edges of the cake at even intervals and push to the bottom of the cake. Rest one iced horse against each piece of dowelling.

Just before you are ready to serve the cake, very carefully place the top cake on top of the dowelling. Serve immediately.

The perfect cake for a party with a witches and wizards theme. Try to find magic candles that re-light to complete the spooky theme.

spooky spell book

1 quantity Extra Large Basic Chocolate Cake (page 11)
1 quantity Medium Basic Vanilla Cake (page 11)
1 quantity Chocolate Fudge Frosting (page 15)
½ quantity Buttercream (page 14)
black writing icing
silver writing icing
edible silver balls
orange sprinkles and edible glitter
assorted Halloween sprinkles

33 x 23 x 6-cm/13 x 9-inch cake pan, greased and baselined with greased baking parchment
piping bag, fitted with a star nozzle/tip
piping bag, fitted with a small, plain nozzle/tip

SERVES 20

Preheat the oven to 180°C (350°F) Gas 4.

Make the Chocolate Cake mixture and spoon into the prepared cake pan. Bake on the middle shelf of the preheated oven for 45 minutes, or until a skewer inserted into the middle of the cake comes out clean. Leave the oven on. Let the cake cool in the pan for 10 minutes before turning out on to a wire cooling rack. Turn the cake the right way up and let cool completely.

Clean the cake pan, then grease and baseline it again. Spoon in the Vanilla Cake mixture and bake on the middle shelf of the preheated oven for 30 minutes, or until a skewer inserted into the middle of the cake comes out clean. Let the cake cool in the pan for 10 minutes before turning out on to a wire cooling rack. Turn the cake the right way up and let cool completely.

Use a long, serrated knife to level the top of the chocolate cake if necessary. Cut it in half horizontally to make 2 pieces of even thickness. Lay one piece of cake on a serving board and spread with 4–5 tablespoons of the Chocolate Fudge Frosting. Top with the

vanilla cake, spread with 4–5 tablespoons of the buttercream and cover with the second layer of chocolate cake. Cover the top and one long side of the cake (the spine of the book) with chocolate frosting, spreading evenly with a palette knife.

Fill the piping bag (with the star nozzle/tip) with the remaining buttercream and pipe 'pages' on the remaining 3 sides of the book, leaving a narrow border. If you don't have a piping bag, spread the buttercream with a palette knife and drag the tines of a fork through it to create the effect of pages.

Fill the second piping bag with the remaining chocolate frosting and pipe an edge all around the top and bottom of the book, filling in the border you left around the buttercream.

Using black writing icing, draw spiders and their webs on the cover of the book. Draw a wizard's hat and decorate with silver writing icing, edible silver balls and orange sprinkles.

Sprinkle orange glitter over the book and scatter Halloween sprinkles around the book on the serving board.

The cupcakes and chocolate-coated cones for these hats can be prepared in advance and assembled on the day of the party. Try to find a good selection of ghoulish sweets and candies to fill the cones with.

wizards' hats

1 quantity Large Basic
   Chocolate Cake (page 11)
300 g/10 oz. dark/
   semisweet chocolate,
   roughly chopped
18–20 ice cream cones
edible silver balls
1 quantity Chocolate Fudge
   Frosting (page 15)
assorted sprinkles
assorted candies

*2 x 12-hole muffin pans,
   lined with 18–20 silver
   or gold foil cases*

MAKES 18–20

Preheat the oven to 180°C (350°F) Gas 4.

Make the Basic Chocolate Cake mixture and divide between the foil cases. Bake on the middle shelf of the preheated oven for 20–25 minutes, or until a skewer inserted into the middle of the cupcakes comes out clean. Let cool in the pans for 10 minutes, then transfer to a wire rack to cool completely.

Melt the dark/semisweet chocolate in a heatproof bowl set over a pan of barely simmering water (do not let the base of the bowl touch the water). Stir until melted and smooth, then remove from the heat.

Hold an ice cream cone over the bowl of chocolate and pour the melted chocolate over with a spoon until the cone is evenly coated, allowing any excess chocolate to drip back into the bowl. Scatter with edible silver balls, then stand the hats upright on a tray and let set.

Cover the top of each cupcake with a swirl of Chocolate Fudge Frosting and scatter assorted sprinkles over the top. Fill the chocolate-coated ice cream cones with candies and stick one on top of each cupcake.

For the best results make the cake parts of this recipe the day before the party. They can then be frosted in advance on the day and the final assembly completed about an hour before serving. Fill with sweet treats of your choice.

pirate's treasure chest

1 quantity Extra Large Basic Vanilla or Chocolate Cake (page 11)

1 quantity Small Basic Vanilla or Chocolate Cake (page 11)

1 quantity Chocolate Fudge Frosting (page 15)

sugar-coated chocolate drops

red liquorice shoelaces or similar

gold- and silver-covered chocolate coins

assorted 'jewel' candies

24 x 12-cm/9 x 5-inch loaf pan, greased and baselined with greased baking parchment

a piece of stiff card, cut slightly smaller than the base of the loaf pan

cocktail sticks/toothpicks

SERVES 10–12

Preheat the oven to 180°C (350°F) Gas 4.

Make the Extra Large Cake mixture and spoon into the prepared loaf pan. Bake on the middle shelf of the preheated oven for 1 hour, or until a skewer inserted into the middle of the cake comes out clean. Leave the oven on. Let the cake cool in the pan for 10 minutes before turning out on to a wire cooling rack. Turn the cake the right way up and let cool completely.

Clean the cake pan, then grease and baseline it again. Spoon in the Small Cake mixture (this is for the lid of the treasure chest) and bake on the middle shelf of the preheated oven for 20–25 minutes, or until a skewer inserted into the middle of the cake comes out clean. Let the cake cool in the pan for 10 minutes before turning out on to a wire cooling rack. Turn the cake the right way up and let cool completely.

When you are ready to assemble the cake, place the larger cake in the middle of a large plate or board. Use a long, serrated knife to level the top of the cake if necessary. Spread two-thirds of the Chocolate Fudge Frosting over the whole cake using a palette knife, dragging the knife across the frosting to create a woodgrain effect.

Wrap the prepared card in foil. Spread a little of the frosting over one side of the foil board and stick the cake 'lid' on top. Cover with the remaining frosting. Decorate both parts of the treasure chest with sugar-coated chocolate drops and red liquorice shoelaces.

Position the lid at an angle to the treasure chest and secure with cocktail sticks/ toothpicks. Fill the treasure chest with chocolate coins and 'jewel' candies (which also act as an extra support for the lid).

Let your inner-fairy go wild with the pink on this cake! If you don't fancy making a fairy you could always top the cake with a toy fairy or princess instead.

fairy cake

1 quantity Medium Basic
Vanilla Cake (page 11)
1 quantity Large Basic
Vanilla Cake (page 11)
1½ quantities Buttercream
(page 14)
6 tablespoons raspberry jam
edible silver and white balls
assorted sprinkles
1 large white chocolate
rainbow button or similar

FAIRY
150–200 g/5–7 oz. ready-to-
roll sugar/gum paste
(Regal Ice)
pink food colouring paste
mauve food colouring paste
yellow food colouring paste
black writing icing
sparkly pink writing icing

*20-cm/8-inch and 23-cm/
9-inch round cake pans,
greased and baselined
with greased baking
parchment*
cocktail sticks/toothpicks
*3 piping bags, fitted with
star nozzles/tips*

SERVES 16

To make the fairy for the top of the cake, lightly dust a clean work surface with icing/confectioners' sugar and knead the sugar paste until pliable. Divide into pieces for the body, head, arms, legs, wings, hair and magic wand. Tint the body part pink with food colouring paste (page 17). Tint a little extra sugar paste mauve, roll into stripes and press to the body. Roll out a pair of legs and arms, a stick for the wand and a sphere for the head.

Tint a piece of sugar paste yellow and divide it in half. Use one piece to make a star for the magic wand and stick it to the white wand stick. Cut the second piece into tiny strips for the hair. Very lightly dab the top of the head with a drop of cold water and attach the hair. Use the black and pink writing icing to draw a face on the fairy and to decorate her dress and wings. Let dry on parchment paper for a couple of hours.

When you are ready to make the cake, preheat the oven to 180°C (350°F) Gas 4.

Make the Vanilla Cake mixtures (separately) and spoon the Medium into the smaller cake pan and the Large into the larger pan. Bake on the middle shelf of the preheated oven until a skewer inserted into the middle of the

cakes comes out clean – 30–35 minutes for the smaller pan and 40 minutes for the larger. Let the cakes cool in the pans for 10 minutes before turning out on to wire cooling racks.

Meanwhile, use cocktail sticks/toothpicks to secure the fairy's body parts together. Remember to remove the cocktail sticks/toothpicks before letting children tuck into the fairy.

Divide the buttercream between 3 bowls and tint one pink, one mauve and leave the last one plain. Fill each piping bag with a different colour of buttercream.

Use a long, serrated knife to level the tops of the cakes if necessary. Cut each cake in half horizontally and sandwich back together with a couple of tablespoons of the raspberry jam. Sit the larger cake in the middle of a large plate and top with the remaining jam, then the smaller cake. Pipe buttercream rosettes over the tops and sides of both cakes in alternate colours. Scatter with edible balls and assorted sprinkles.

Sit the fairy on top of the large white chocolate rainbow drop in the middle of the cake just before serving.

The shortbread or gingerbread recipe will make more crowns than you need to decorate the cake but any extras can be served alongside so that each child has their own cookie.

princess crown

1 quantity Extra Large Basic Vanilla Cake (page 11)
1 quantity Glacé Icing (page 15)
1 quantity Gingerbread Shapes (page 12) or Shortbread (page 13), baked into crown shapes
assorted writing icing
edible silver balls
1 quantity Buttercream (page 14)
edible red glitter
1 white chocolate rainbow button or similar

2 x 20-cm/8-inch round cake pans, greased and baselined with greased baking parchment
ribbon (optional)

SERVES 10–12

Preheat the oven to 180°C (350°F) Gas 4.

Make the Vanilla Cake mixture and divide between the prepared cake pans. Bake on the middle shelf of the preheated oven for 35–40 minutes, or until a skewer inserted into the middle of the cakes comes out clean. Let the cakes cool in the pans for 10 minutes before turning out on to wire cooling racks.

Meanwhile, carefully spread Glacé Icing over the crown shapes with the back of a spoon. Let set for at least 2 hours. Use writing icing to pipe multi-coloured dots over the crowns and to draw outlines. Stick silver balls to the icing. Let dry for a further hour.

When you are ready to assemble the cake, use a long, serrated knife to level the top of one of the cakes. Place it on a serving plate and spread 3 big tablespoons of the buttercream over the top. Put the second cake on top, rounded side up.

Cover the top and sides of the cake with the rest of the buttercream, spreading evenly with a palette knife. Sprinkle the top of the cake with the red glitter. Stick a white chocolate rainbow button in the middle of the cake. Tie a ribbon, if using, around the bottom of the crown, then stick the crown cookies around the outside of the cake.

For this castle you will need three cakes baked in the same square pan. Two of the layers form the base of the castle and the third layer is used for the turrets. Use either the Meringue Frosting (page 15) or Buttercream (page 14) to cover the castle. I have made this a fairy-tale castle but by swapping the white frosting for Chocolate Fudge Frosting (page 15) it could be turned into a fortress. Use chocolate bars to make a drawbridge and dark chocolate to cover the cones.

fairytale castle

3 quantities Large Basic
    Vanilla Cake (page 11)
6–8 tablespoons raspberry
    jam
1½ quantities Meringue
    Frosting (page 15) or
    Buttercream (page 14)
edible silver and pink balls
diamond-shaped candies
mini pink and white
    marshmallows
red liquorice shoelaces
    or similar
150 g/5 oz. white
    chocolate, chopped
5 ice cream cones
assorted sprinkles

*20-cm/8-inch square cake
    pan, greased and
    baselined with greased
    baking parchment*

SERVES 20

Preheat the oven to 180°C (350°F) Gas 4.

Make one quantity of the Large Cake mixture and spoon into the prepared cake pan. Bake on the middle shelf of the preheated oven for about 35 minutes, or until a skewer inserted into the middle of the cake comes out clean. Leave the oven on. Let the cake cool in the pan for 10 minutes before turning out on to a wire cooling rack. Turn the cake the right way up and let cool completely. Clean the cake tin, then grease and baseline it again. Repeat the step above twice more with the remaining mixtures.

Use a long, serrated knife to level the tops of the cakes if necessary. Place one cake on the serving plate, spread with 2 tablespoons of the jam and top with the second cake.

Refer to the diagrams on page 21. From the third cake cut out 2 x 8-cm/3¼-inch rounds (with an upturned glass if necessary) and 4 x 5-cm/2-inch squares. Place a square on each

corner of the castle and secure with a touch of jam. Sandwich the round pieces together with jam and place in the middle of the castle.

Working quickly, cover the castle with Meringue Frosting or buttercream, spreading evenly with a palette knife. Decorate with the silver balls, diamond-shaped candies and marshmallows. Cut the liquorice shoelaces into a door shape and stick to the frosting.

Melt the white chocolate in a heatproof bowl set over a pan of barely simmering water (do not let the base of the bowl touch the water). Stir until melted and smooth, then remove from the heat. Hold an ice cream cone over the bowl of chocolate and pour the melted chocolate over with a spoon until the cone is evenly coated, allowing any excess chocolate to drip back into the bowl. Scatter with sprinkles, then stand the cones upright on a tray and let set. Place a cone at each corner of the castle and one in the middle.

This cake seems complicated but it just requires patience. You need to make paper templates before you get started. The cake keeps for 3–4 days in a dry place. Make it the night before to let the icing set.

hansel & gretel house

700 g/5⅓ cups plain/all-purpose flour

1½ teaspoons bicarbonate of/baking soda

a pinch of salt

4 teaspoons ground ginger

3 teaspoons ground cinnamon

275 g/2 sticks plus 2 tablespoons unsalted butter, diced

150 g/¾ cup (caster) sugar

125 g/½ cup soft light brown sugar

225 g/1 scant cup golden/light corn syrup

4 large egg yolks, beaten

2 quantities Glacé Icing (page 15)

chocolate rainbow buttons, flaked chocolate bar, candies and sprinkles

TEMPLATES
roof: 23 x 15 cm/9 x 6 inches; larger walls: 20 x 15 cm/8 x 6 inches; side walls: 15-cm/6-inch square topped with equilateral triangle 15 cm/6 inches across and 10 cm/4 inches high

piping bag, fitted with a star nozzle/tip
solid baking sheets

SERVES 10–12

Sift the flour, bicarbonate of/baking soda, salt, ginger and cinnamon into a large bowl. Put the butter, sugars and golden/corn syrup in a saucepan over low heat. Stir from time to time until the sugar has dissolved and the butter has melted. Remove from the heat, pour into a bowl and let cool for 10–15 minutes. Make a well in the dry ingredients and pour the cooled sugar mixture into it. Add the egg yolks and mix with a wooden spoon until the dough comes together smoothly. Divide into 2 even pieces, flatten into a disc, wrap in clingfilm/plastic wrap and chill for 2 hours.

Preheat the oven to 180°C (350°F) Gas 4.

Divide one of the gingerbread discs into 3 equal pieces. Place one piece on a sheet of baking parchment. Lightly dust a rolling pin with flour and roll out the gingerbread into a rectangle about 4 mm/⅛ inch thick. Using the roof template as a guide, cut out a rectangle. Write 'roof' on the parchment so that you can identify the piece later. Transfer to a baking sheet and bake on the middle shelf of the preheated oven for 15 minutes, or until deep golden and starting to darken at the edges. Repeat with another piece of gingerbread, making one of the larger walls. Use the remaining piece to make one side wall. Repeat with the other gingerbread disc. You should now have 2 of everything.

As each section comes out of the oven lay the relevant template over the section and trim the edges with a long knife. Cut out the windows and doors (reserving the piece for the door). Let cool on the baking sheets.

Fill the piping bag with the Glacé Icing. Cover any unused icing with clingfilm/plastic wrap. Take the front section of the house and pipe a thin line of icing along the bottom edge. Stand this on a serving board and hold upright with a jam jar on either side. Pipe icing along the bottom and sides of one side wall and stick together with the front. Repeat with all the walls, holding them in place with more jars for at least 30 minutes until the icing has set firm.

Pipe thin lines of icing across each roof panel and stick chocolate rainbow buttons on to them to cover the roof. Let set for at least 15 minutes. To attach the roof, pipe a length of icing along the top edges of the house and put the roof in place. Hold together for a few minutes. Pipe another line of icing along the top of the roof and under the eaves to secure. Pipe icing along the edges of the roof, letting it drip into icicles. Use any remaining icing to decorate the doors and windows. Stick the door in place slightly ajar. Stick the flaked chocolate in for the chimney and decorate all over with candies and sprinkles.

I have made this a three-layer cake but if you have two 20-cm/8-inch pans you could easily make an Extra Large quantity of Basic Vanilla Cake and divide the mixture between the pans. In this case, the cooking time for the cakes will be a little longer. This cake will keep in an airtight container in a cool room for up to 2 days.

box of secrets

3 quantities Medium Basic
  Vanilla Cake (page 11)
4 big tablespoons raspberry
  or apricot jam
½ quantity Buttercream
  (page 14)
1 kg/2 lbs. ready-to-roll
  sugar paste (Regal Ice) or
  fondant icing
pink food colouring paste
yellow food colouring paste
blue food colouring paste

20-cm/8-inch square cake
  pan, greased and
  baselined with greased
  baking parchment

SERVES 16

Preheat the oven to 180°C (350°F) Gas 4.

Make one quantity of the Medium Cake mixture and spoon into the prepared cake pan. Bake on the middle shelf of the preheated oven for about 30–35 minutes, or until a skewer inserted into the middle of the cake comes out clean. Leave the oven on. Let the cake cool in the pan for 10 minutes before turning out on to a wire cooling rack. Turn the cake the right way up and let cool completely. Clean the cake pan, then grease and baseline it again with greased baking parchment. Repeat the step above twice more with the remaining mixtures.

Use a long, serrated knife to level the tops of the cakes if necessary. Place one cake on the serving plate, spread with 2 tablespoons of the jam and top with the second cake. Spread with the remaining jam and top with the final cake layer. If necessary, trim the sides of the cake to make them completely straight.

Cover the top and sides of the cake with the buttercream, spreading it evenly with a palette knife. Refrigerate for ½–1 hour.

Cut off one-third of the sugar paste, cover with clingfilm/plastic wrap and set aside. Lightly dust a clean work surface with icing/confectioners' sugar and roll the remaining sugar paste into a square roughly 45 cm/18 inches across. Loosely drape the sugar paste over a rolling pin and use to lift up over the cake. Using your hands, smooth the sugar paste over the top and sides of the cake. Trim off any excess from the bottom with a knife.

Divide the reserved sugar paste and any trimmings into 3 parts and tint each part with a different food colouring paste (page 17). Dust the work surface with icing/confectioners' sugar again and roll out the coloured sugar paste. Cut into strips ranging in width from about 1–4 cm/⅜–1¼ inches. Stick to the cake to resemble ribbons using either a little water, or some leftover buttercream. Set aside to dry for at least 3 hours before serving.

The cake, flower shapes and gingerbread people can all be prepared in advance for this cake. If you prefer, you could frost the cake with Buttercream (page 14) rather than Meringue Frosting (page 15).

merry maypole

1 quantity Large Basic
   Vanilla Cake (page 11)
1 quantity Glacé Icing (page 15)
1 quantity Gingerbread Shapes
   (page 12), baked into small
   and large people
200 g/6½ oz. sugar/gum paste
   (Regal Ice) or ready-to-roll
   royal icing
assorted food colouring pastes
3 tablespoons raspberry jam
1 quantity Meringue Frosting
   (page 15)
1 stick of rock/candy stick
1 regular marshmallow
1 mini marshmallow

*2 x 20-cm/8-inch round cake
   pans, greased and baselined
   with greased baking
   parchment*
*piping bag, fitted with a fine
   writing nozzle/tip*
small shaped cookie cutters
*baking sheets, lined with
   baking parchment*
assorted ribbons

SERVES 10

Preheat the oven to 180°C (350°F) Gas 4.

Make the Vanilla Cake mixture and divide between the prepared cake pans. Bake on the middle shelf of the preheated oven for 30 minutes, or until a skewer inserted into the middle of the cakes comes out clean. Let the cakes cool in the pans for 10 minutes before turning out on to wire cooling racks.

Meanwhile, fill the piping bag with Glacé Icing and use to decorate the gingerbread people. Let set for at least 2 hours. Reserve any leftover icing for later.

Divide the sugar/gum paste into 4 parts and tint each part with a different food colouring paste (page 17). Dust a clean work surface with icing/confectioners' sugar and roll out the coloured sugar paste no thicker than 2 mm/1⁄16 inch. Stamp out into different shapes with the cookie cutters. Place on the prepared baking sheets and let dry overnight.

When you are ready to assemble the cake, use a long, serrated knife to level the tops of the cakes if necessary. Place one cake on a serving plate, spread with the jam and top with the second cake.

Working quickly, cover the cake with the Meringue Frosting, spreading evenly with a palette knife. Stick the royal icing shapes all over the sides of the cake.

Tint the remaining glacé icing with any of the leftover food colouring pastes and use to pipe dots around the shapes.

Secure the ribbons to one end of the stick of rock/candy stick using sticky tape. Push the regular marshmallow, then the mini marshmallow over the top of the rock and push the other end into the middle of the cake. Arrange the gingerbread people around the edge of the cake, pushing them gently into the frosting to make them stand up.

wildlife

Make the daisies at least a day before you plan to serve this cake to allow them to dry and harden. They will keep for up to one week in an airtight container.

daisy patch

500 g/1 lb. sugar/gum
   paste (Regal Ice)
yellow food colouring paste
1 quantity Large Basic
   Vanilla Cake (page 11)
1 quantity Buttercream
   (page 14)
green food colouring paste

daisy-shaped cookie cutter
baking sheets, lined with
   baking parchment
cocktail stick/toothpick
23-cm/9-inch round cake
   pan, greased and
   baselined with greased
   baking parchment
piping bag, fitted with
   a star nozzle/tip

SERVES 10–12

Set aside 50 g/2 oz. of the sugar/gum paste and cover with clingfilm/plastic wrap until needed. Dust a clean work surface with icing/confectioners' sugar and roll out the remaining sugar/gum paste no thicker than 2 mm/¹⁄₁₆ inch. Stamp out into daisy shapes with the cookie cutter. You will need 30–40 flowers and any trimmings can be re-rolled. Arrange on the prepared baking sheets. Rest some of the daisies against a wooden spoon so that they have a gentle curve.

Tint the reserved sugar paste yellow with the yellow food colouring paste (page 17) and roll into small balls for the insides of the daisies. Flatten each ball slightly and prick the surface with a cocktail stick/toothpick. Very lightly brush the middle of each daisy with a drop of cold water and stick one yellow ball to the middle of each flower. Let the finished daisies dry for 24 hours.

When you are ready to assemble the cake,

preheat the oven to 180°C (350°F) Gas 4.

Make the Vanilla Cake mixture and spoon into the prepared cake pan. Bake on the middle shelf of the preheated oven for 35 minutes, or until a skewer inserted into the middle of the cake comes out clean. Let the cake cool in the pan for 10 minutes before turning out on to a wire cooling rack. Turn the cake the right way up and let cool completely.

Using a long, serrated knife, cut the cake in half horizontally to make 2 pieces of even thickness. Place the bottom layer on a serving plate and spread with 3–4 tablespoons of the buttercream. Top with the second layer. Tint the remaining buttercream bright green with the green food colouring paste and spoon into the piping bag. Cover the top of the cake with buttercream rosettes and pipe lines up the sides of the cake to resemble blades of grass, covering it completely and evenly. Stick the daisies all over the top.

Popular with younger children, this cake is a cinch to make – everything is done the day of the party and the decorating is very simple.

curly caterpillar

1 quantity Extra Large Basic Vanilla Cake (page 11)
1 quantity Small Basic Vanilla Cake (page 11)
1 quantity Buttercream (page 14)
yellow food colouring paste
red food colouring paste
green food colouring paste
mauve food colouring paste
blue food colouring paste
liquorice shoelaces
16 jelly beans
2 sugar-coated chocolate drops
assorted writing icing

1-litre/4-cup, 650-ml/ 2⅓-cup and 2 x 350-ml/ 1½-cup ovenproof glass bowls, greased and dusted with flour
6-hole muffin pan, lined with paper cases
2 green pipe cleaners

SERVES 10–12

Preheat the oven to 180°C (350°F) Gas 4.

Make the Vanilla Cake mixtures (separately) and divide the Extra Large between the prepared bowls and the Small between the paper cases. Bake just under the middle shelf of the preheated oven until a skewer inserted into the middle of the cakes comes out clean – 45–55 minutes for the larger bowls, 30–35 minutes for the smaller bowls and 20–25 minutes for the cupcakes. Let cakes cool in the bowls or pan for 10 minutes before turning out on to wire cooling racks to cool completely.

Use a long, serrated knife to level the bottoms of the cakes if necessary.

Divide the buttercream between 5 bowls and tint each one a different colour with the food colouring pastes (page 17). Bear in mind that the quantity of buttercream needed for each cake will differ depending on the cake sizes.

Cover each cake a with different colour of buttercream, spreading evenly with a palette knife.

Peel the paper case off one cupcake (and freeze the rest of the cupcakes). Cover the cupcake with buttercream. Arrange all the cakes on a serving board in a curly caterpillar shape and in decreasing size of cake.

Cut the liquorice shoelace into 17 x 5-cm/ 2-inch lengths and position in pairs on either side of each cake as legs. Stick the last length of liquorice to the largest cake at the front of the caterpillar as a mouth. Position the jelly beans on the ends of the legs as feet. Stick the sugar-coated chocolate drops above the mouth for the eyes and stick the pipe cleaners in the top for the antennae.

Use the writing icing to spell out the child's name along one side of the caterpillar and to add more decoration, if desired.

117

Coloured pipe cleaners are readily available in craft stores and make great antennae for all manner of critters. If you don't want to make up a whole batch of cupcakes you could always use a storebought cake for the ladybird's head.

lucy ladybug

1 quantity Large Basic
   Vanilla Cake (page 11)
1 quantity Small Basic
   Vanilla Cake (page 11)
1 quantity Buttercream
   (page 14)
red food colouring paste
black food colouring paste
1 long liquorice shoelace
giant chocolate buttons
2 yellow sugar-coated
   chocolate drops

*2-litre/quart ovenproof
   glass bowl, greased and
   dusted with flour*
*6-hole muffin pan, lined
   with paper cases*
2 red pipe cleaners

SERVES 8–10

Preheat the oven to 180°C (350°F) Gas 4.

Make the Vanilla Cake mixtures (separately) and spoon the Large into the prepared bowl and divide the Small between the paper cases. Bake just under the middle shelf of the preheated oven until a skewer inserted into the middle of the cakes comes out clean – 40–45 minutes for the cake and 20–25 minutes for the cupcakes. Let the cakes cool in the bowl or pan for 10 minutes before turning out on to wire cooling racks to cool completely.

Use a long, serrated knife to level the bottom of the cake if necessary.

Put three-quarters of the buttercream in a bowl and tint it red with the red food colouring paste (page 17).

Tint the remaining buttercream black.

Place the cake, flat side down, on a serving plate and cover with the red buttercream, spreading evenly with a palette knife. Stick the liquorice shoelace along the middle of the body and arrange the chocolate buttons on either side.

Peel the paper case off one cupcake (and freeze the rest of the cupcakes). Level off the domed top. Cover the cupcake with the black buttercream, spreading evenly with a palette knife, and place it upside down on the plate against the ladybug's body.

Stick the yellow sugar-coated chocolate drops on the head for the eyes and push the pipe cleaners on top as the antennae.